# CRIMINAL CONFESSIONS

## What Goes on in the Mind of a Criminal?

Psalm 32:5

ADRIAN MAURICE JENKINS

First Edition



**Case ID:** 1-14352799601

# Dedication

First and foremost, I thank my Lord and Savior, Jesus Christ, who is the head of my life and made it all possible. Secondly, to my beloved mother, father, siblings, relatives, and friends, living or dead. Lastly, to all of the many men and women who are either doing time, have done time, or have come to terms with their wrongs. It is to all of you that I affectionately dedicate this book to each and every one of you.

# Table of Contents

# FOREWORD

This book has been constructed from a penological perspective, and because of this, it has been prepared with much patience and diligence. Its goal is to try and discourage others from making the same regrettable mistakes as so many of us have made, which led to us serving time as a result of those choices. It has been said that "A wise man will learn from other people's mistakes, whereas a fool would fail to learn from his own mistakes." However, our past mistakes are good at times; they are how we learn and grow and give us the experience we need in life because it is our past that enables us to draw from our "good and bad" experiences when ministering to others. My purpose for such a book is to try to influence others to think before they act as to the long-term effects that any immoral action may cause further down the road. And my thanks go out to each of the men (who wish to remain anonymous) but who have shared their stories for this purpose in part 1 of the book.

Proverbs 28:13 says, "He who covers his sins will not prosper. But whoever confesses and forsakes them will have mercy." As a contribution to humanity, we hope that by sharing these stories, they will help to open the eyes of mainly the youths of society today who are being constantly sent here to fill these prisons. So many of them began to feel a sense of obligation. There are more and more youths that are as young as fifteen years old who are ignorant of the consequences of certain crimes and the severe sentence that can be imposed for being committed, such as armed robbery, aggravated assault, etc., which in some states such as Georgia can carry up to a minimum sentence of ten years to life. Becoming convicted of such can leave a young man/woman with a criminal record while losing their youth and ultimately have a negative impact on their future. And it is not our wish to just sit here in prison and let our fate become their fate! Because one of the most profound influences that our children face in life is the pressure to concur with other youths even when they suspect that their decision to do so is wrong.

With at least 70 percent of the US prison population consisting of young men ranging from the ages of nineteen to twenty-five, this book serves as a reminder of the illegal activities that lead anyone to prison. And it is my hope and prayer that its message speaks to all readers, young and old alike, because every experience, however bitter, has its lesson. And as mentioned above, the enemy here is ignorance, and therefore, it is essential that we succeed in our effort to convey the value of one's freedom. We shouldn't be so quick to judge others when we've all made mistakes. And indeed, a simple mistake can turn into a tragedy at any given moment. But rather, let's allow the mistakes of others, no matter how big or small, to become life lessons to us all. For as you will find in John 10:10, I'm convinced that Jesus can provide salvation, forgiveness, and abundant life to even those of us whom Satan has managed to lead astray. For if God is for us, then who can be against us?

"A man must be big enough to admit his mistakes, smart enough to profit from them, and strong enough to correct them!" (john C. Maxwell).

Each individual's name has been changed from their birth name throughout this book in an attempt to protect their true identities (with the exception of those deemed necessary).

# PART 1

## Crimes and Their Consequences

My name is Augie; the crime that led to my imprisonment occurred in 2002. Being high on crack since the earlier part of the day and having spent what little money I had to obtain the drug. By nightfall, I found myself strolling along the metro streets of Atlanta, Georgia, flat-broke yet craving drugs. I've never done anything like what I had begun to contemplate at that moment. And why I chose to listen to the thoughts that entered my mind that night to this day is still a mystery to me. I mean, I had been using crack at the time for a few years and had experienced cravings before, but never had I dreamed that my desire to use the drug would someday influence me to commit a crime. You see, I had entered a Hard Rock Café one night, which was mostly occupied by whites who seemed to drink more and, as a result, became more wasted as opposed to the other races, making them a far easier target for what I had in mind.

However, the very next thing that I knew, I was awaiting a victim in a nearby ally at around 11:30 p.m. When shortly after, a Caucasian male, who appeared to be staggering, made his way toward the alleyway in which I was waiting. As he continued to draw near me, my adrenaline began to race. It somehow seemed to fuse my courage even though I was extremely nervous. But as he neared me, unaware of my presence, I leaped from the shadows unexpectedly, drawing him into the semidarkness where I awaited. With a knife in hand, I said to him, "I don't want to hurt you. So just give over your money, and you won't get hurt!" Pulling his wallet from his pocket, I then conducted a swift search of the remaining ones, but finding no funds in them, I shoved him aside and fled. Swiftly, I had covered about two blocks when, wouldn't you know it, A police car pulled across my path as I crossed the street. The cop hastily exited his vehicle with weapon drawn, demanding that I cease all movement. I was arrested.

And after spending nearly six months in confinement, I learned through my state-appointed attorney (lawyer retained by the state) that there had only been $20 in the wallet that I'd taken but never got to spend! The police had driven upon me within moments of my having committed this immoral act. I never got the chance to even search the wallet to see how much may have been inside it or even to get rid of it. I received a maximum sentence of twenty years, ten of which to be served in prison, with the remainder to be served on probation following my release from prison for the offense of "armed robbery." I received a year, nevertheless, for each dollar that I had taken but never got to spend, and I have been incarcerated for nearly six years with a discharge date set for 2022.

It's mandated in the state of Georgia, however, that all violent offenders must serve 65 to 95 percent of their sentence before even being eligible for parole. Nevertheless, I have put someone's life in danger, and it was wrong, and by sharing my misdeeds, I am looking for neither sympathy nor pity, but rather to remind anyone that one mistake can sometimes carry a very severe penalty! A price that, in the end, you wouldn't want to pay! And if I may end my admission on a positive note, then it would be to advise everyone that drugs hinder ambitions and ultimately destroy dreams! So, I would like to caution you that you should never think that you are an exception if ever tempted or pressured to experience drugs. Or to become involved with them in any way!

*****

My name is Kevin, and the story that led to my incarceration occurred in 2004. It involved a woman who the victim and I were both having an affair with. I first came in contact with Sandra in a nightclub during the winter of 2003, and we became acquainted. Sandra informed me that she was involved with someone but that maybe we could still get to know one another. I accepted, and we exchanged numbers.

Over the next few months, Sandra and I became very intimately involved, going out to dinner movies and having sex regularly. It had gotten to the point that I had begun to ask her to break it off with James, who was already in her life upon my meeting her, and to move into my place with me. I informed her that she had captured my heart, and as a result, I wanted her in my life completely. Sandra agreed that she would inform James that she was seeing someone else and no longer wished to continue the relationship, but on the day that she had done so, James, who, being in a rage, threatened that she would regret her decision to ever leave him for another man. However, it wasn't long after the threat that, as anticipated, Sandra moved into my place. And having learned of the threat, I armed myself for Sandra's protection, though I wished that it wouldn't have resulted in this. My very first encounter with James, however, occurred at my home. I informed him as humbly as possible that his presence wasn't welcomed and that he should vacate the property and never return. But not until uttering threats and words of profanity did James enter his vehicle and depart, but only to return a week following the encounter.

James made the fatal mistake of returning to my place. I wasn't home, of course, but Sandra was. James, who, after a forced entry into my home, had severely attacked Sandra. I arrived home following the incident after having received an urgent call from

Sandra to do so. I entered the apartment only to find her swollen, bruised, and crying. Once informed of who was responsible for the assault and forced entrance, my initial impulse was to retrieve my nine-millimeter and storm out of the apartment in search of James. But in spite of my overwhelming desire to do so, I knew I must postpone the impasse at least long enough to first ensure Sandra's well-being, but if I could turn back the hand of time, I would definitely have done things differently. Plainly put, I would have involved the authorities as opposed to what I had done! After getting Sandra admitted at the local hospital, I drove my car nonstop in search of James. Eventually, I located his vehicle, and I parked my car out of view of the area as I awaited his arrival. And sure enough, James wasn't long in appearing as he headed toward his vehicle, unaware of my presence. Stepping from between the two vehicles where I had been secretly awaiting, I drew my firearm and began to fire. I squeezed off a total of five shots. An act that can't be undone, and one in fact that, in the end, I can't help but regret! The medical examiner revealed that James died from three bullet wounds to various parts of his body. And the consequences I am left to live with are life in prison and the constant reminder of having taken someone's son, brother, nephew, uncle, and perhaps father away from them forever! And in this prison, I die mentally with each passing day. In closing, I would like to encourage everyone to embrace their freedom because you may never truly realize its value until you have lost it!

*****

My name is john, and the crime that led to my imprisonment involves the illegal sale of narcotics in 2003. I have been a drug dealer since the age of fourteen. Being raised in a single-parent home in the projects wasn't easy! There were many nights that my sister and I went to bed hungry, and let me tell you that sleep doesn't come easily when one is hungry. And I can't say which bothered me the most during those heartbreaking times, my very own hungry pains or the late-night crying of my little sister. Our father walked out of our lives when my sister was only two years old and with me being eight. I've struggled for many years to forgive him, and truth be told, I don't think I could ever bring myself to do so. My mother was a beautiful, loving woman who neither drank nor used drugs and always did the best she could to provide for my sister and me. She did not deserve to be deserted by him and forced to raise us along.

When I turned fourteen, I began to sell marijuana for an "OG" in the hood. This at least enabled me to aid my mother in the welfare of my sister, myself, and, of course, her. And it wasn't long thereafter that, against her will, I eventually dropped out of school and became a full-time hustler. And by the age of fifteen, however, I began to sell crack cocaine. The money was fast and addictive, but the streets, on the other hand, were cold and dangerous. There was once when I had a gun placed to the back of my head, and the gunman demanded that I hand over both my drugs and cash. This encounter only encouraged me to begin carrying a concealed weapon of my own for my protection in the streets. I had decided that I was not going to risk my life and freedom just to be robbed and killed, unarmed. Because as I have stated, money is fast and addictive! And I had no intention of stopping!

Now, seeing my little sister have enough to eat, wear new clothes, and have money in her pocket was all that mattered to me. So I continued selling drugs and was eventually able to relocate my mother out of the projects and into her very own four-bedroom home, although she never came to terms with my way of getting money out of genuine concern for my well-being. I was eventually able to persuade her, nevertheless, to accept my offer to purchase for her the home in the amount of $110,000 in a residential area of the suburb. I love my mother and sister more than my very own existence, and because I was able to accomplish a somewhat more comfortable life for them, I do not regret my fate, which, unfortunately, sometimes results from this lifestyle how I desperately wanted nothing more than to see her live life a little easier. But the truth of the matter is that being in prison is the price that sometimes, sooner or later, will accomplish this momentary fame of being a drug dealer.

I also managed, however, to establish a savings account for my sister's college years, which I placed in my mother's name to ensure her the education that I never got. And please understand that I am in no way bragging about having done these things. But it is just that in doing them, I've achieved what mattered most in all of my gaining. I must also consider the numerous people whom my drugs have affected. Addicts whose potential has been hindered or altogether destroyed due to the poison I distributed. Not to mention the children whose parents were addicts who oftentimes would go as far as to sell their food stamps and other such things just to obtain the drug, and I must admit that it was always this realization that reminded me of what a true "lowlife" I had been a drug dealer.

It grieved me and would break my heart with each transaction I made, but for selfish gain, I continued to sell the hazardous substance. And what do I have to show for it after being busted for the second time, paying excessive amounts to attain a lawyer, and basically financing my personal necessities while being incarcerated for the past nine years in prison? Well, I am virtually spent! That's right! I have been reduced from being a once-upon-a-time "kingpin" to just enough prison statistic!

I am presently serving a twenty-year sentence in the Georgia Department of Corrections for the crime of trafficking (second offense). I am now thirty-five years old, with a maximum discharge date set for 2024. And my advice to the young men and women who may be experiencing hard times and are contemplating drug dealing as a means of survival is to please seek other alternatives instead! Although money is fast, you must realize that what usually comes easy also goes easy! Not to mention the danger involved in becoming a drug dealer that may cost you your life! So please seek instead an education, degree, or profession which could ensure you true success. And always remember that you are the designer of your destiny. That you are the author of your story, which is the life you live in this world!

*****

My name is Nathaniel, and what led to my imprisonment was the crime of rape in 2001. I was seventeen years old at the time of committing this gruesome act against another human being, for which I not only regret but also feel overwhelmed with remorse. My victim is a seventeen-year-old female, who I will refer to as Brenda, who happened to be home during my attempted burglary, seeing how my plan had been only to enter the home and take a few possessions and split. But as I arrived at the home while thinking no one was inside, I approached the rear of the house as a better choice of entry, and once inside, confidence that no one was home, I advanced further into a nearby bedroom where I began to search for valuables.

When I realized at this time, I wasn't the only one present in the home! Shocked at the sound of someone's presence and unaware of who it was, I eased from the bedroom in an attempt to exit the home when, to my surprise, I saw her! Brenda was in the kitchen removing items from the refrigerator, and her attire had been nothing more than panties and a bra. I was mesmerized by the mere sight of her, and when suddenly she turned, dropping the dish in alarm of my presence, the offense was committed of which I will not get into the graphic details. However, I was arrested five days later.

To avoid the possibility of life in prison, which is the penalty for a crime of rape in the state of Georgia, I pleaded guilty to a sentence of twenty years in prison. I have now been incarcerated for thirteen years, and what was intended to be a simple burglary turned out to be a gruesome act of violence against a young, innocent woman that I am now left to live with because here I sit in prison reflecting on the error of my way a mistake that I would now have to live out the remainder of my life forever regretting! But through my story, nevertheless, I embrace this opportunity to apologize to my victim for the physical, emotional, and psychological drama that I've caused her. I take full responsibility for my immoral actions as I seek her forgiveness through prayer.

*****

My name is Robert, and I am incarcerated for the offense of forgery, which I committed in 2010. I was nineteen years old at the time. A native of Alabama, I resided in Atlanta, Georgia, in 2001 in the hopes of a new beginning. The product of a broken family, I have had to defend as well as provide for myself since the age of sixteen. My mother was mentally impaired, and my father was abusive and a drug addict. I left home at the age of sixteen even though I had no place to go, had no money, and was too young to work, so my first battle was with homelessness, and I quickly resolved to shoplifting as a means of survival. But little did I know then that this petty lawlessness of mine was only the beginning of what would eventually send me to prison!

I was eighteen years old when I resided in the ATL, where I took refuge in one of the homeless shelters around the city. And with no criminal record at the time other than the time or two that I had been caught shoplifting, which is a nonindictable offense (misdemeanor), I pursued work in the form of construction, which, after about two months of steady search, it became clear to me that all of the job sites that I had encountered had no interest in hiring a "black man," not as long as there was plenty of Mexicans and Caucasians needing jobs as well.

What convinced me of this was the mere fact that at each construction site that I had ventured to, you could count the number of black men employed there on one hand, even though they were building skyscrapers. Frustrated and with little hope of ever obtaining employment, I ceased searching. My only means of cash had been from the sales of food items that I would purchase off of my debit card (food stamps) and sold to the men in the shelter, which had barely afforded the train and bus fair that I'd purchase to travel from one job site to the next. And being destitute in a city such as Atlanta, which is overpopulated with beautiful and attractive women, a man's pride is easily wounded when he is unable to embrace his independence. When everywhere you travel throughout the city, you're going to see tons of exciting babes whose appearances are not only breathtaking but also intimidating.

Then you know that somehow, you have got to elevate your status! So one day, when an SUV pulled up to the curb and the occupants asked if anyone cared to make a wad of money, I agreed that I was interested, even though it involved them counterfeiting several company checks in my name. At this point, I was still without a job, homeless, and in desperate need of the $500 or more that they said I could make. I had known of these guys recruiting people from all over the metropolitan area for some time, but never before had I been interested nor had the courage to get involved until now.

The scheme was simply to carry the checks into the bank while looking presentable and remaining calm. And so, on the following day, I participated in the scheme and was successful in cashing three checks that earned me $750, and boy, was that money needed! However, I attempted to succeed in this illegal scheme about a month later but only to find myself locked inside a bank while being restrained by two guards until the police could arrive; I was arrested and later convicted for the crime of forgery, which earned me ten years in prison. Prison is designed to give a man sufficient time to contemplate the error of his ways, but some prisoners don't experience a reality check until much later, regardless of how much time they have spent in prison up until they do. Because sadly, it takes some to become released and then come back again and again before realizing that the grass is truly greener on the other side of the fence!

*****

My name is Jimmy, and what led to my prison term was the crime of murder in 2009. I was seventeen years old at the time of the crime being committed and had never been involved with the law in any way prior to the incident. I was in the eleventh grade and very much involved in sports as a wide receiver on my high school football team. My future was bright, and I was optimistic until one day, it changed my entire life! I was using marijuana on the "down low," although I would never use it before practice or during practice, nor during or before a game, but nevertheless, this negative habit of mine has proved to be my downfall!

My sister Teresa had been involved in a relationship with a fellow by the name of Steven, whom she had started out with as being friends for about a month or so before becoming involved with the guy. So, neither of us had truly known Steven as well as we assumed that we had in such a short time span. Steven also used marijuana, and he and I would occasionally indulge in the drug. So one day, while Steven was visiting Teresa, he asked me if I had any, and after stating that I did not, he suggested that we both make a trip by the dope man spot to get a sack. He stated that the purchase of the drug would even be on him, for the both of us. And so we departed, and upon our arrival, Steven passed me $50, suggesting that I make the cope. After exiting the car and climbing the flight of stairs leading up to the dope man's apartment deck, it was then that I noticed that Steve had also exited the vehicle and was now making gestures for me to wait for him. And once that I had been approached by Steven, he quickly informed me of his plans to rob the drug spot. But as I immediately informed him that I wanted no part of it, Steven withdrew a Glock semiautomatic weapon that he kept secured underneath of his coat and aimed it at my chest.

At a loss for words, I obeyed the instructions to knock at the door and waited nervously for someone to answer when a voice that I recognized as a female named Amanda asked, "Who is it?" I announced my presence, and the door was immediately opened by her, only to find Steven's pistol pointed at her face as he shoved me forward into the front room. Taking hold of Amanda's arm, he demanded to be led quietly to the dope man through the apartment. And as we reached a room where there were people gathered, drinking, talking, and using drugs, they hadn't even noticed our presence until we had entered the room. Taken by surprise at what was obviously about to go down, the dope dealer reached out for his firearm, which had been resting on a nearby nightstand, but before he could retrieve the weapon, Steven's Glock had ranged off like a cannon, hitting him in the chest, neck, and in the forehead, killing him instantly.

The frantic and hysterical onlookers began to panic but quickly regained their composure as Steven then placed the barrel of the gun to Amanda's head and threatened to pull the trigger. And as everyone fell silent, I was then ordered by him to search everyone, to deprive them of their jewelry and cash, which, out of fear for my life, I obeyed. And having gathered these things along with the drugs, we exited the apartment with no further casualties being committed. However, I was arrested, charged, and later convicted of murder and armed robbery in spite of my innocence or the fact that I had voluntarily gone to the police station to report what had occurred within hours of the incident and that my involvement had been completely forced at gunpoint.

I have been sentenced to prison for life for a crime that I was forced into committing. Even the victims believed that my involvement had been voluntary, which mostly led to my conviction. And soon after my sentence had begun, I contemplated suicide, but thanks to the love and support of my family, I am no longer suicidal! But instead, I have come to embrace each day one day at a time while remaining optimistic. I've since learnt that at least in 2004, for instance, the Bureau of Justice Statistics, Drugs, and Crime Facts reported that 17 percent of state prisoners and 18 percent of federal prisoners said they committed their current offence to obtain money for the drugs. And this doesn't include the prisoners that are incarcerated for selling drugs. But perhaps the users who needed money in order to purchase the drugs.

So, a very high percentage of prisoner's crimes are, in fact, in some way, drug-related. I am now twenty-one years old and would like to caution the youths in society today that it would be wise not to allow yourselves to become involved with using or dealing drugs at any time because drugs, for one thing, destroy ambitions! But if you are already into them, then do yourself a favor and quit because I would hate to see my fate become your fate, which is why, perhaps, parents should always remain attentive when it comes to their children's interests.

*****

My name is Rickie, and the immoral act that sent me to the slammer (prison) was aggravated assault and domestic violence in 2005. I was twenty-eight when I got involved in an affair with a woman who was thirty-seven years old at the time. Jackie and I had shared an apartment together and had been in an affair for a period of two years prior to the incident that led me to prison. We both drank, although I wouldn't consider us to be alcoholics, and were outgoing. The only problem was that Jackie just couldn't seem to hold her liquor at times and, as such, would oftentimes humiliate me in public. For instance, there was once while visiting a friend who had invited us to a cookout, and after having a great time for the two hours that we had been in attendance, my mood began to change as Jackie clearly became more and more intoxicated. Approaching her, I stated, "Baby, I'm tired. Let's go home," and before I realized it, Jackie had slapped the cap that I was wearing clean off my head, which went flying across the yard while loudly stating that "I go when I'm ready to go. Until then, leave me the hell alone!"

Humiliated by this, I knocked her to the ground right before someone intervened. But there had been other occasions such as this that have provoked me into putting my hands on Jackie, which has resulted in arrests and restraining orders against me. But in spite of our seemingly constant fighting, whenever she would allow her liquor to overcome her, we would always remain a couple. However, the cause of my imprisonment involved my cousin, Frankie. I had allowed him to stay with Jackie and me, which was only meant to be for a little while since he claimed to have fallen on hard times.

Soon after taking him in, I went to a bar one night with a friend where we had been drinking and socializing with a few others until around midnight. It was then that I decided to return to the apartment, and upon my arrival, after letting myself in, I couldn't believe what my own eyes were seeing. There they were, Jackie and Frankie, being so occupied in their lovemaking that they hadn't even bothered to notice me entering the apartment. I grabbed hold of Frankie and shoved him to the floor as I warned him that it was best that he gather his few belongings and get out ASAP if he knew what was best for him. But it was after that Frankie had gathered his things and left that I really lost all control.

I had taken Jackie by the hair and dragged her over to the closet, where I retrieved an old wooden oak cane. Taking the cane into my hand, I began to strike Jackie repeatedly until she appeared to be unconscious. Realizing what I had done, I dialed 911 before departing in the night. Jackie was hospitalized for a period of six weeks as a result of the beating. She'd sustained several cracked ribs, a broken jaw, and a wrist. And I was arrested four days after my brutal attack against Jackie and eventually convicted and sentenced to ten years in prison. Though there have been times when I've tried to convince myself that my actions were normal under the circumstances I encountered at the time, which caused me to lose it, in my heart, I know I was wrong and should have reacted differently.

If you are abusive in your relationship, then you should end the abuse because it would be best if the both of you should depart rather than end up hurting the one you love!

*****

My name is David, and in the year of 2009, I committed the crime of domestic violence and manslaughter. I was sixty-four years old when I met Victoria, a young mother of three, who was seventeen at the time of our meeting. In spite of our age difference, when I first encountered Victoria, I was instantly drawn to her. Although I had never spoken to her, I only admired her from a distance. But on the second occasion that I saw her, I approached her in the hope of getting to know her. Victoria shared with me during our first encounter that she lived with her mother and that she had three kids. She further informed me that she was not involved with anyone and that age was not a factor. So I asked if maybe we could exchange phone numbers as I admitted my infatuation with her, which she didn't seem to mind or to have a problem with. So the two of us began to become more acquainted over the phone during the next few weeks, by which I learnt that she recently had her own apartment but was forced to move in with her mother because of her struggles to finance the bills, which became too much to bear.

Victoria went on to stress how she truly enjoyed the independence of being on her own, yet she had nothing against the quality time that being back at home with her Mom afforded her. But that being a woman, she'd much rather embrace her independence. I suggested that maybe she would like to move in with me since I owned my own house in which I lived alone and wouldn't have minded providing for her and the children, but I was asked by Victoria if I would allow her time to think it over. I advised her to take as much time as needed but just to know that my doors were open to her, and it wasn't until about a month after we had discussed it that Victoria decided to take me up on my proposal during a phone conversation.

A few days after I made her and the children welcome into my home, Victoria and I discussed our expectations of each other prior to her moving in, and the first three months of her stay were truly wonderful. We spent a great deal of time together doing things we both shared a mutual interest in, such as going out to dinner, having a cookout in the yard, and watching movies, to name a few, but it wasn't long after the first three months that Victoria's interest in the nightlife begins to cause me discomfort.

She would say that she was going out with peers, and I would tell her to have a good time but that I would appreciate it if she didn't come in too late, which she swore that she wouldn't. But more and more, Victoria had begun to go out, and she would return later and later. It had gotten to the point where we rarely spent time together anymore. So I decided to confront Victoria about my dislikes, and we quarreled. And it wasn't until a few more episodes of her going out and coming at all hours of the night that she had gone out, as usual, one evening and did not return home until around 3:00 a.m. the following morning. Victoria's children had spent the night at their grandmother's the night before and were not at home the following afternoon because it was about this time that Victoria had awakened and decided to get out of bed.

I approached her about it, and we began to argue when Victoria started to say things that I took to be very disrespectful. And it was at this point that I felt that I had taken as much of her behavior as I would take. So I began to ask her to just leave and not to return except to gather her belongings, but Victoria made no attempts to leave. She only continued to say things that caused me to become angry.

And before I knew it, I had left the room, only to return carrying a nine-millimetre, which I asked her again to leave my home, but she wouldn't, and the next thing I knew, I had raised the firearm and fired it at her, which unfortunately ended her life. I don't know what I was thinking that caused me to do what I have done. It may have been jealousy, the thought of eventually losing her to a younger man, that led to it. But what I do know is that I never meant to harm her! I called 911 right after realizing what I had done. I requested an Ambulance, but sadly, Victoria expired before reaching the hospital! I pleaded to her death and received a twenty-year sentence to serve in prison. I have now turned sixty-eight, and at the duration of my sentence, I'd be eighty-four years old, which is set for the year 2029.

I don't expect to live this long, considering my declining health, and quite frankly, the thought of dying in prison doesn't upset me for feeling like this is where I should die for the regrettable act that I've committed! There is simply no excuse! I can only pray that God will forgive me as I attempt to express how truly sorry I am to Victoria's family and children!

*****

My name is Nathan, and what led me to prison was a bank robbery in 2007. I was a heroin addict at the time, and robbing a bank was something I had never ever thought of doing, let alone attempting to pull off! Although I've committed other crimes prior to doing so, I've done nothing ever of this magnitude! On the day of doing so, I took a piece of paper after deciding that the use of a "weapon" would only make the consequences that much more severe if I'm caught in the act. And I scribbled a note stating, "This is a robbery." I then nervously made my way into the bank at around noon because there would be customers throughout the bank at this hour of the day. So I cautiously entered the bank so as not to draw attention to myself while I scoped the extent of security before attempting to carry out my plan.

Contented with the seeming lack of security, I made my approach toward the teller as I swiftly handed over the note that read, "This is a robbery! Place hundreds, fifties, and twenties in the bag. Do as the note says, and you won't get hurt!"

The bank teller looked up at me as if to ask, "Are you serious?" but my demeanour must have said it all because it was at this point the teller hastily began placing the bills into the bag, doing so in a manner as to not draw attention to the situation. I took the bag and casually made my exit as I was both nervous and frightened of being caught! But I knew that any chance of my succeeding with this robbery depended wholly on my ability to remain calm, cool, and collected. And amazingly, I was able to exit the bank without incident and make a clean getaway with a little over eight grand!

Unfortunately, though, with being a heroin addict, even this sum of money doesn't last long when snorting it in a powder form as opposed to banging it with a needle. It only took me three weeks to waste the money, after which I attempted to pull off a second bank robbery, which I seemed to have pulled off the first time so easily, but only to discover that my luck didn't last long! I was caught in the act and eventually convicted and sentenced to ten years in prison. I was never linked to the first robbery, however. My discharge date is set for 2017, and my advice to anyone who may be struggling with a drug addiction is to please seek help if it is what is needed in order to overcome your addiction!

*****

My name is Wallace, and the stupidity that led to my predicament of incarceration has to do with armed robbery, which occurred in 2003. I was only seventeen years old when I committed the biggest mistake of my life while trying to "fit in with the tough crowd" in my neighbourhood and school. In order to become a member of the gang (organization), which I prefer not to identify, one had to prove that he is worthy of becoming such. And some initiations required that you undertake a severe beatdown to become affiliated, which is known as "blood in" and "blood out!" Or that a vicious act of violence is committed by you against someone that could sometimes also include the destruction of their property.

In my case, however, it had been the latter. I was given a firearm after being instructed what to do to the identified victim, where to commit the act, and when to carry it out! And now that I look back on this, I can't believe how fascinated I must have been with the thought of becoming a gang member to have done such a thing. After accepting the firearm, I entered a convenience store at around 9:30 p.m. as I had been instructed, and there were four members of the gang who were awaiting my return with the dough about a block away from the store, which I was to rob. Before entering, I waited until the store was unoccupied with customers.

After entering, however, I approached the store clerk and asked for a pack of Newport cigarettes while placing a five-dollar bill onto the counter, and as he reached over his head for my selection, it was then that I removed from beneath my waistband the.32 revolver, which I had been given. Aiming the weapon at the clerk's head, I demanded the money, and just as he reached for the cash register and began collecting the money, three customers entered the store, with one approaching the counter where the robbery was in progress.

Instinctively, I lowered my weapon out of the view of the customer, and before I realized what a critical mistake it had been, the clerk reacted and withdrew from beneath the cash register a.44 Magnum. In disbelief, there I stood, dumbfounded at the instant change of events! The clerk ordered me to lower my weapon to the floor and to place both hands in the air while now having his weapon aimed at me. Afraid to risk any foolish attempts to regain control of the robbery, I slowly lowered my weapon to the floor as directed when the clerk leapt over the counter and kicked it to the side; he then asked one of the three customers to "call 911!"

I was arrested and later convicted and sentenced to fifteen years in prison for the crime of armed robbery and have a maximum discharge date set for the year 2018. I've discovered that prison life is congested with gang activity, and as such is the cause of my imprisonment. My fascination with it, however, died upon my arrest! And my advice to every young man and woman is to be yourself and to know that the hero that we sometimes seek in other's lives is within each of us! Godspeed!

*****

My name is Brian, and my current predicament is all derived from a crime of aggravated stalking and aggravated assault by the use of a motor vehicle in 2007. The crime involves my ex-wife, Regina, who had been my high school sweetheart since junior high. And although we are no longer a couple, it is with her that my heart resides. Right after graduation, however, we married, and two years later, our adorable daughter, Audrey, was born. And I must admit that this had to be the most nervous yet exciting day of my life!

After graduation, I took up employment at RadioShack as a clerk. Regina, on the other hand, had become employed at Macy's as a saleswoman, and our combined incomes afforded us not the best but a comfortable life in the suburb. But at the age of twenty-five, seven years after we married, I began to drink, and as my drinking escalated, the more intolerant I seemed to become. Regina had strongly disapproved of my drinking while adding that it had somehow changed me from the person that I once was. But the more she would complain, the more in denial I was about it.

First, it was the verbal abuse, which was quickly followed by the physical abuse. And if this wasn't bad enough, then there was the cheating, sleeping around with other women, and coming in all hours of the night. There was even once when Audrey was preparing to do the laundry that she'd discovered on the shirt that I'd been wearing during the night before that it not only smelt of another woman's fragrance but also there had been lipstick near the collar, and after revealing the shirt to me, instead of manning up to my wrong, we fought, after which she gathered a few clothes, took our daughter and angrily left in tears for her mother's. Regina had taken our daughter six months prior to discovering the shirt with the fragrance and lipstick on it and left me before returning home three weeks after leaving me. That situation had regarded a text message she'd discovered in my phone. But this time was different. Regina had gone and filed for a divorce and has been staying at her mother's place for the past five months now. I had tried desperately to win her back, but she had in spite of my efforts, gone and had the court issue a restraining order against me. She had also ceased to answer any of my calls and refused to allow me to meet with her to discuss the matter of divorce.

So one day, I was under the influence of alcohol when I spotted Regina coming out of a convenience store at around noon as she headed for her vehicle, and in a moment of drunken inspiration, I entered my pickup truck and began to pursue her in spite of the restraining order. But as I followed her, I did so at a safe distance and remained undetected of her for miles before finally driving upon her on an isolated road. I began to blow the horn as I gestured for her to pull over. Peering into the rearview mirror and realizing that it was me who attempted to stop her, Regina refused to stop the vehicle. Accelerating the truck, I began to ram the rear bumper of her vehicle, which caused it to swerve, but she managed to maintain control of it. I rammed it a second time, sending the vehicle swerving further to the shoulder of the road, which, in order to prevent entering the ditch, Regina stopped the car.

Pulling up next to her, I healed up a.38 revolver while yelling through the window that she was going to make me kill her! And threatening her life was something that I had never done before. Terrified. However, Regina slammed the vehicle into reverse and accelerated it backwards before making a complete U-turn and heading back toward town. At this point, I decided to no longer pursue her, but instead to go home and sleep the liquor off while never once thinking that Regina would have gone to the authorities with regard to my pursuit of her. The police obtained a search warrant and arrived at my residence within a matter of hours of my pursuit of Regina had occurred and had awakened me. They retrieved the firearm, which I had placed underneath the truck seat, and apprehended me on the spot. Talking about a rude awakening!

I was arrested and denied bail for not only failing to comply with the court's order but for having done so in such a violent way as to nearly run Regina off of the road while driving at a considered speed. I've been sentenced to ten years in prison with a discharge date set for the year 2017, and now I realize what a fool I've been, having lost the love of my life to alcohol and to a woman whom I had no true feelings for compared to the one I had for my wife! I've also lost the opportunity to watch my daughter grow up day by day and be the kind of father that she deserves. There is no doubt that I have failed her, though it is hard to accept! But however difficult, I will remain optimistic in regard to a father-daughter relationship with my child even though the divorce between her mother and I has been finalized.

*****

My name is Adrian Maurice Jenkins, and although I am the author of this book, my story is no different than any of the stories that you have read thus far. One thing, if nothing else, that we all have in common is the fact that we are all currently incarcerated at the time of writing this book. Yet what we have in common is the desire to discourage anyone and everyone from making the type of mistakes that we have made, which have caused us our freedom! Although I've also written my autobiography titled A Journey to Freedom, the Divine Dreamer, I do not feel it would be fair to my fellow prisoners or to the readers if I didn't share my own misdeeds to be included in this book as well.

Let me begin by sharing that I am a native of a very small town called Louise, Mississippi. I was raised by loving parents who both did the best they could to provide for me and my five siblings and to teach us moral principles. It was around the age of fourteen that I began to experiment with drugs, and it was marijuana that had been my first experience until the age of nineteen that I had been introduced to crack cocaine, and my life had never been the same.

As Robert had done, I, too, had resided in Atlanta, Georgia, in the year 2001, pursuing a new beginning where I took up refuge in a homeless shelter following my release from prison in Mississippi in 2000. My first ambition had been to obtain employment, of course, but after what seemed to result in a useless search for employment, I became depressed with being destitute, which ultimately led to my relapse, and I am a victim of long-term adult drug abuse as a result of my addiction to crack cocaine. Now, I see every temptation I face as an opportunity to conquer its strength, which only makes me that much stronger in the Lord. Nobody is perfect! The past is the past, and it can't be undone.

We all have sinned and did things we're not proud of. My story and past are no different. But always remember that you will never know how strong you are if your strength is never challenged. I truly believe that sometimes it's the worst experience in life that can help us the most, like me being sentenced to serve a term of ten years in prison for the crime of shoplifting, which was connected to my crack addiction, by which I was convicted of my attempt to take $260 worth of clothes, which also included several watches and sets of hair clippers.

There is one good thing, if nothing else, that has come from my many years of confinement: I now understand and see so many things, mainly in life, very clearly. God's grace has truly been sufficient in my life, and His strength perfected in my times of weakness. And seeing how His grace is a free gift, then I am forever indebted to His mercy! You see, even when I didn't fully believe in myself or believe that things would ever change in my life for the better, and when people saw only the worst in me and said that I would never amount to anything, God saw the best in me! That which He would cause to manifest through me, and He never once forsaken me nor left me in the hands of the enemy! So please understand that we don't have to be held captured mentally by our current circumstances or our past, but to know that God is only using us in our times of conflict for His good purpose and plan for our lives. Godspeed!

# PART 2

## Prison Life

Now we all know that a story is best told from the inside as opposed to telling it from the outside looking in! And it is through my eyes that I make this attempt to show you, the readers, the harsh reality of prison life. But first, I would like to point out that there are roughly forty different prison settings throughout the state of Georgia. And the inmate population in each of these prisons varies from 1,100 to 1,300 men. With the exception of a few states, such as Texas and California, Georgia has the next highest rate of imprisonment. What you may not know is that more taxpayers' money is being spent on the operation of these prisons than on the essential necessities of our government-run schools.

Now that I've shared some of the crimes that bring people to prison let's look at what life is like inside prison. I mean, things such as what a convict may have to endure just to survive from day to day because, in prison, the tension, stress, and frustration are always in the air. I mean, you have to always maintain awareness of your surroundings if you are to survive.

There is virtually no privacy in prison, with the exception of solitary confinement! This is where a prisoner is placed alone in a cell, but even then, the only thing that separates you from the next prisoner is the wall in between your cell and his/hers, where you are subjected to such cruel conditions as being only allowed to shower "three days" per week, where you will only be permitted to exit your cell for recreation one hour per day, where television, etc., is not permitted (as opposed to the general population), all while remaining confined to an eight-by-twelve cell.

There's a convict I've met after being placed into one of these isolated cells next to Georgia State Prison. Mike was a black male who had been convicted and sentenced to life in prison for the crime of murder. Now the infamous Georgia State Prison, however, had originally been built as a "high max" security prison many years ago where, in fact, the electric chair had been administered to execute prisoners. And it had also been the prison where the movie The Longest Yard, starring Burt Reynolds, was filmed. However, Mike had been incarcerated at the time that I met him for a total of twenty-six years, which began in the year 1987, and had spent the last seventeen of those years in Georgia State Prison in one of those isolated cells.

Mike wasn't exactly what the system may have considered being a "modern-day prisoner" by far. But after being incarcerated for so many years, nevertheless, the parole board had decided to set Mike a parole date, at which time they anticipated paroling him. But before his parole date could arrive, Mike had gone and caught himself in an "assault on an officer" charge by fracturing the officer's wrist. The prison officials had taken Mike to Free World Court in their pursuit of Free World charges being brought against him. This resulted in the DA making Mike an offer of five additional years to be served in prison in exchange for a guilty plea. However, Mike refused the plea while maintaining his claim that he had been provoked by the officer who had led to the incident. At the same time, knowing that doing so would have meant that he would not only have had to serve the mandatory five-year sentence consecutively from his current sentence. But entering such a plea would have definitely ruined any chance of him making his upcoming parole date.

However, after his parole date had finally occurred and he realized, nevertheless, that he wasn't being paroled, Mike had his family intervene who had been informed by the parole board that not unless the pending charge is resolved in Mike's favor, then his parole has been put on hold otherwise. After researching the prison law library, Mike learned that the statute of limitation only allowed four years for the court to try him on the pending charge, which began at the time that the incident occurred. Otherwise, failing on the court's behalf to do so results legally in the dismissal of the charge, and the court had been procrastinating on moving forward with the case, leaving them with only eleven months remaining of the four years to do so, at my last consulting with Mike. And let me tell you that most correctional officers do, in fact, abuse their authority like once when, I witnessed an inmate who was in the process of being relocated by correctional officers from one dormitory (housing unit) to the dorm where I was located through the window of my cell, who had all been white males. The dormitory at this time wasn't an isolation dorm, however, but rather a segregation dorm, meaning that it was unlike the eight-by-twelve cell that Mike had been confined to for the past seventeen years. As opposed to isolation, there is one man assigned to a cell; in segregation, there are two.

I stood there observing the actions of these officers. I had watched them escort the inmate up to his assigned cell in the new location, and once positioned outside of the cell's door with the inmate being handcuffed from the back, I watched as the sergeant, who was the highest-ranking officer of the three, knock on the cell's window, awakening the sleeping inmate that occupied the cell, who was without a cellmate. He then ordered him to step forward to be handcuffed so that his new cellmate could enter the cell. Because by the prison's policy, whenever an inmate has been placed in "isolation or segregation," he/she must first place both hands/wrists out through the "tray-flap" to be handcuffed from the back before officers are authorized to open the cell door. So whenever an inmate is removed from his/her cell for whatever reason, whether it's for medical purposes, recreation, law library, visitation, etc., he/she must first be restrained before the cell door opens. The only exception to the policy is when an inmate refuses to cooperate, requiring force to be used against the inmate.

As the inmate that was in the cell approached the cell door, he was to be cuffed by the officers as ordered. I noticed him peeping out of the cell's window before complying. This, however, enabled the newcomer to observe the inmate that was occupying the cell, and having done so, he immediately informed the sergeant, "Me and this guy are enemies."

To which I heard the sergeant reply, "I don't care. You're going in the cell!"

"But if I'm placed in the cell with this guy [both of the inmates were black], someone is bound to get seriously hurt!" stated the inmate.

The sergeant ignored his plea to not be placed in harm's way; instead, he began to gesture toward the control booth for the officer operating it to open the cell door, and after that, he handcuffed the inmate in the cell. As the inmate that stood on the outside of the cell, having one of the other two officers gripping the chain of the handcuffs that had him bound from the back, began to shift himself opposite the cell entrance, the officer gripping the chain of the cuffs became aggressive and started to yank the chain to force the inmate to the direction of the cell door as he harshly demanded that he remain still. They had begun to argue before the sergeant, who was the ranking officer, and he had decided to take control of the heated moment, took hold of the chain, and then forced the inmate to face forward against the wall.

Now, with the sergeant having positioned himself behind the inmate, he then began to yell into the inmate's ear, "You're going in the cell!" While the inmate was expressing his refusal to be placed in harm's way without putting forward any physical resistance, I observed that the sergeant, for no legitimate reason, took the palm of his hand and, with no warning, pushed the back of the inmate's head into the concrete wall three swift times, causing his face to make contact with it, which on the third blow, sent blood streaming down his face from the deep gash that he'd sustained to his forehead, and the last that I heard of it was that the inmate had filed a lawsuit requesting for him to be compensated against the brutality and to have the sergeant terminated.

I've been transferred to a different prison since encountering Mike; however, I haven't a clue as to the outcome of his predicament. The vast majority of prison guards appeared to think that just because prisoners are incarcerated, and most of the time out in the middle of nowhere in some remote rural area, they get to come to work and treat prisoners as if they are animals and no longer humans and that there should be no consequences to their injustice. As if having become incarcerated somehow diminishes your humanity!

Now, there are inmates in prison with all sorts of strange nicknames, such as "Cat Fish," "Pork Chop," and "Corn Dog," to name a few. Speaking of which, I spoke with a younger prisoner who spent the majority of his youth in prison. Corn Dog went on to share with the young man that he had been transferred from Georgia State Prison located in Reidsville, Georgia, to Smith State Prison in 2008. He said that he was now sixty years old and had been sentenced to life plus twenty-five years in prison, but for what crime, he did not say. However, he went on to share that he spent all of his thirties, forties, and fifties behind bars, having been imprisoned since the age of twenty-nine. After spending the majority of his youth in prison and now working on his sixties being spent in prison as well, he has now reached the point of giving up on any hope for release. Because every time that he has come up for parole in the past, the parole board has set him off, leaving him with little expectations or ambitions toward release.

Just as Mike had done, this elderly prisoner had also served a significant amount of time in one of those eight-by-twelve cells in isolation, twenty-three years to be exact, while serving time at the infamous Georgia State Prison. If you are still young and are about to be released from prison, then you should realize that you are blessed! Prisoners should always embrace their opportunities to regain freedom, whether it is near or years down the road, for there are many men in prison who have been sentenced to spend the remainder of their lives incarcerated! And this is the message that I perceived and think that the older prisoner was attempting to convey to the younger one. Smith State Prison, however, is where I have been transferred to and is what is known as a "level 5" prison. Its capacity is 1,300 prisoners, with a statistic of 85 percent of said total being sentenced to a "life" or a "natural life" sentence in prison.

Prison, in general, is no more or less than a gigantic human warehouse, a sea awash with criminals of all mentalities, such as murderers, rapists, kidnappers, robbers, drug dealers, drug addicts, etc. And you will even be in the presence of fellow prisoners for many years while sleeping under the same roof as they are and never know what crime they may have committed or what they are capable of.

There was one morning during breakfast in segregation—which is, as all other meals that are served in the lockdown unit, they are delivered to the inmates' cells—that an officer informed my cellmate and me while feeding us our meals of the horrible discovery that they'd encountered while conducting count earlier on that morning. We were told that an inmate had been killed by his cellmate, a twenty-three-year-old black male and that his victim had been a fifty-seven-year-old black male (may his soul rest in peace). The officer said that as the inmate had been questioned, his account of the incident to prison staff had been that the deceased had threatened to rape him. The victim had been found while still lying in the top bunk of the double-bunk beds, which they shared in the cell, as did all other inmates confined to the lockdown unit. While having sustained numerous stab wounds to various parts of his body, from the staff's viewpoint, there didn't appear to have been a struggle between the two prisoners, as it turned out that the perpetrator hadn't sustained a scratch. They speculated that the victim had been brutally attacked by the perpetrator for little or no reason while he lay awake in bed, or worse, while he slept. The perpetrator was immediately transferred to Jackson, Georgia, where he was placed on "high max" and is also where the death penalty is administered to execute prisoners to await trial for the man's death.

History truly does repeat itself. Because ironically, a similar occurrence transpired around the year 2007 in the DeKalb County jail in Decatur, Georgia. This incident also involved a young black male who was in his early twenties and the victim had been an elderly black male; both inmates were cellmates confined in segregation at the time. As in the first instance, this elderly prisoner (may his soul rest in peace) had also been in his mid-sixties when he was discovered by correctional officers while conducting security rounds lying in his bunk, deceased from numerous stab wounds inflicted by the perpetrator. It was described by the officer, as I could imagine, as being a horrific and heartbreaking sight. But this perpetrator, too, was known to have mental health issues. However, had also been charged with the old man's death, nevertheless, and later convicted and sentenced to the death penalty, where he awaits execution.

On February 12, 2013, in Smith State Prison, there was also an incident that, unfortunately, claimed the life of a young Hispanic man (may his soul rest in peace) who was around the age of twenty-three years old at the time of his death. It was about a month before this incident occurred that we were all being confined to the lockdown unit, two men to a cell. My cellmate and I occupied cell number 238, while the young victim and his cellmate, who was also a Mexican somewhere around the age of forty, occupied cell number

240. I did not know either of these guys personally due to our twenty-three to twenty-four-hours-a-day lockdown status, even though we remained in nearby cells for a period of three months before I was relocated to the unit next door. But during our stay in close proximity, they both used to pass by my cell while being escorted by the officers during the days of the week when showers are conducted in the lockdown unit. This, however, enabled me to observe both of these men and while living in very close proximity to them, never once did I ever observe any commotion among them. In fact, they both appeared very humble in spite of my observation of the elderly Mexican who would oftentimes be sharpening a homemade knife on the concrete nearly every time we would be allowed to go outside for an hour-a-day recreation, Mondays through Fridays.

Being confined to the lockdown unit, inmates are to remain segregated, so when we are permitted yard call, we are handcuffed, each man from the back, and then escorted one cell at a time out to the yard, which consisted of fenced-in cages, which only you and your cellmate would occupy. And these fenced-in pens each have concrete floors, and it would be during these times in the yard that I would occasionally observe the older Mexican scrubbing his homemade knife against the concrete. Although this action could have served as a warning sign to the young Mexican that maybe he should have requested to be separated from his cellmate, on the other hand, unless you and your cellmate were actually having personal conflicts among yourselves, then this mere action of the perpetrator wouldn't have seemed to be in the least bit out of the ordinary in prison.

However, it was approximately one month after I had been relocated to the building next door that I was informed of the tragic news of the young Mexican's death. On the day of his untimely death, an officer had handcuffed the victim while both men were still inside their cell from behind his back. But no sooner when the younger Mexican had become secured in restraints had the elderly Mexican produced his weapon (homemade knife) and began stabbing his victim repeatedly, who, being bound by the handcuffs from the back, was totally helpless to defend himself. I never learnt exactly what the actions of the officer that had handcuffed the victim may have been to the unexpected horror, which unfolded right before his very eyes other than reporting it over the radio. Nor had I learnt exactly what may have triggered the elderly Mexican to commit such a horrific act against the younger one other than it being said that it was a case of mental health issues on behalf of the older Mexican.

But what I did learn, however, is that the younger Mexican expired in the cell right where he had fallen before medical personnel could even arrive and remove him from the cell; such was the extent of his injuries. And I must admit that it truly grieves me to have to write of such instances, but nevertheless, it just goes to reflect the harsh reality of prison life and the truth of an earlier statement that I've stressed, which is "You may be sleeping under the same roof as another inmate and haven't a clue as to what crimes he may have committed or what he may be capable of committing."

Violence, however, is a common reaction in prison. It doesn't take much to lose your life or to become beaten unconscious in prison. For instance, due to the high cost associated with utilizing the prison phone system, a great deal of inmates who are fortunate enough to purchase one have obtained cell phones. Now, it is not permitted for prisoners to possess such devices in prison, which are mostly smuggled into the prisons by prison guards and sold for as much as $350 per phone, which is usually just a $14 flip phone from Walmart with a touch-screen phone of any brand costing a prisoner as much as $800 to a $1,000. But although inmates are paying many times over the retail price for these phones, the advantage of owning one under the circumstances makes it worse. So these phones, though cheap in quality, are very expensive and valuable to a prisoner, and it is because of the huge profits involved that prison guards regularly smuggle the drugs, phones, and cigarettes into the prisons for which many are often caught, terminated, and later prosecuted.

But are the phones valuable enough to die for? Well, there was one instance that involved a young inmate who was a gang member affiliated with a gang known as the GDs (Gangster Disciples). However, this inmate (may his soul rest in peace) strong-armed a cell phone from another prisoner who was a Muslim of the Islamic faith and who did not waste any time in informing his community of having been robbed by the GD gang member. Early one morning, as the perpetrator had exited his dormitory to go and receive his insulin medication, little did he know that the Muslims were awaiting his arrival! So, as he strolled alone along the prison compound, unaware of the danger that awaited him, numerous Muslims suddenly appeared seemingly out of nowhere as they surrounded him in an enclosed location of the prison compound from the front and the rear him. They begin to tie the gates shut with bed sheets that they had brought with them for this very purpose, to prevent any possibility of his escape. And with nowhere to run and no one to help him, he had been left alone to face the consequences of his actions.

As the result of several stab wounds to various parts of his body, he expired right where he had been caught; it goes against the "convict code" to steal from other convicts while incarcerated! Although it wouldn't be wise to do so, there are a great deal of inmates who occasionally do, but the repercussions can sometimes prove fatal! Mostly, it would be inmates who lack the support of family members who have not received their account books a single cent since being incarcerated for many years. And as a result, they cannot utilize the prison commissary to purchase such things as chips, sodas, soups, cookies, cosmetics, coffee, cigarettes, etc., which results in a great percentage of these inmates strong-arm robbing other inmates of their store goods. Those who they consider prey!

And an inmate that is more likely to fall victim to prey, however, would be, first and foremost, one who is not affiliated with a gang, one who is up in age, or who appears to be a loner, or one who may even be a Christian! For instance, there was one occasion that I shared with an inmate named Bruce, who had had such an experience. It was told by him that when he first arrived at Smith State Prison after being transferred from another facility, he had been assigned to "H-building," which consisted of two dormitories, an H-1 and an H-2. The dorm's capacity is a total of 108 men, each consisting of fifty-four two-men cells. But unlike isolation, as I have shared, inmates confined there are being locked down from twenty-three to twenty-four hours a day. H-building, which Bruce is referring to, is a general population unit where inmates are only locked in their cells during the hours of 11:30 p.m. until 5:00 p.m. with the exception of weekends when inmates are not locked down until 1:30 a.m.; otherwise, they are free to roam the dorm to watch television, exercise, socialize, etc.

Well, Bruce, being a newcomer assigned to the H-2 dorm, had entered his new environment open-minded and humbled. Six days prior to the incident, since entering his new location, all he did from the time he awakened was sit at an unoccupied table and concentrate on seeking his freedom through the legal writing that he did on his own behalf. He had not been familiar with anyone in the dorm from the time of his arrival, nor was he a gang member. In fact, he had been a forty-nine-year-old black male who had been perceived as "prey" for all the obvious reasons. However, on the seventh day after he arrived in the unit, he purchased for himself $60 worth of commissary items delivered to the inmates in the dorm, and after collecting his products, he headed for his cell. He informed me that he had been inside his cell with the door shut just long enough to have placed the majority of the items into the locker box when two prisoners entered his cell unannounced and quickly closed themselves inside the cell with him with their knives drawn. Shocked, he asked them, "What's the meaning of this?"

Which one of them replied, "You know what it is, Pops. The store goods, hand them over!" And after staring at them as if to say, "It won't be that easy," and having his vibes perceived, he was then warned, "Please don't make us bloody you up, Pops! Niggas got life up in here!" one of them stated. After sizing the situation up and realizing that they had the ups on him, he said to them, "You mean to tell me that y'all have come in here to take my stuff at knifepoint with me being an elderly black man when you have Mexicans and Caucasians out there?"

"Man, we don't want to hear that Martin Luther King sh——!" one of them yelled as the other quickly agreed. And this statement, Bruce figured, only confirmed the ignorance of these two men. And as such, he knew that they were well capable of carrying out the very threat they made toward him, so he declined all impulses to resist but attempted instead to pacify them. So he removed his pillow from its pillowcase and said to them, "Listen, I have a good heart. If y'all wanted some of this stuff, all you had to do was ask, and I would have shared some of it with you," he said as he began to place food items into the pillowcase. But after he had placed about $8 worth of food products into the pillowcase, one of the perpetrators had taken the pillowcase from his hands while stating, "You're moving too slow! Give me the bag!" Having taken the pillowcase, combined with the "bag" that they had brought with them, they had taken the elderly prisoner's entire $60 purchase with no remorse, which included his new shower shoes and hygiene products!

Within an hour of the incident, he informed an officer of having been robbed and that he wished to be relocated to a safer dorm while refusing the officer's request to identify the robbers as it goes against the "convicts' codes" to involve officers in the affair of convicts. The information provided, however, did result in the removal of Bruce to a safer housing unit established for the forty-five-year-old and older. But as for the $60 in commissary items, it was never returned because of Bruce's refusal to identify the perpetrators. And it had been best, nevertheless, that he escaped the ordeal with his life and no property than with neither!

I have seen those in prison who have lost their lives for a lot less! Bruce was one of the few inmates who didn't just accept their prison sentence "innocent or not" without seeking some legal ground that could possibly set them free. And especially if you are innocent! They dedicate themselves to learning the law in their pursuit of freedom. And I recall him stating to me once, "In learning the law, you must also learn to respect the law. Because if you learn the law yet fail to respect it, then it will be the very law that helped you regain your freedom that will send you back to prison!" Statistics have it that 76 percent of all prisoners end up back in jail within five years of being released.

And one terrible example of a prisoner returning to prison shortly after being released occurred in the case of an inmate who, prior to his release, had vowed to do so for his anticipation of getting out of prison with one goal in mind. The goal was the murder of his child's mother, which he fulfilled, and he is now sitting in the county jail, awaiting his return back to prison for her murder, who wanted to get on with her life by being involved with another man while he was serving time.

It was said that he had chopped the woman's body (may her soul rest in peace) in pieces for which he has since been sentenced to life plus twenty-five years in prison, which makes you wonder just how could a human being anticipate such a horrific act against his own child's mother while already sitting in prison, having sufficient time to reconsider the thought, yet failing to do so, when clearly, there was nothing to be gained by it. And he hadn't been released any longer than it had taken him to take the woman's life.

Each morning, when the cell doors would open, you'll find yourself in a day room of a maximum of 107 other prisoners, most of which are from different gangs: Crips, GDs, Bloods, Ghost-face, etc., which would include a small number of non-affiliated inmates who, to the vast majority of the gang members, would be considered as prey for most of the gangs to rob, which doesn't include all gangs or gang members who would seek to take advantage of the weaker or most vulnerable prisoners. But nevertheless, because of the potential danger that is associated with prison life, every day is spent walking around with a homemade shank (homemade knife) while praying that the day will not be the day that you lose your life or are forced to take the life of someone else's to save your own. Because in prison, you would encounter some of the most conceited, arrogant, and heartless people, which includes prisoners and staff alike.

In prison, it's always best to stay in good physical combat shape because you never know just when you may have to defend yourself. And if necessary, never hesitate to throw the first punch because it may make all the difference in the outcome of the fight. Because in throwing the first punch, your intentions should always be to connect with your component with all the gusto that you can muster to eliminate any possible chance of him returning the blow. And if you just happened to fail in putting his lights out, then you want to at least have connected with a solid enough punch to leave him unresponsive while looking up at you, dazed and wondering what day of the week it is!

Hostility breaks out frequently between rival gangs, and shortly after my arrival here at Smith State Prison in Glennville, Georgia, a dispute broke out between two gangs. The dispute occurred one day when the gangs both had been admitted to yard call (recreation) and had erupted into a physical bloodbath within minutes of having exited the buildings. The two gangs involved had been the GFs-Mafias, further known as the Good Fellows, and a gang known as the Bloods. The GFs, however, were acknowledged by the warden as being a notorious and ruthless gang that terrorized the prison.

Upon my arrival here at the institution, I learned that the warden had recently gone throughout the prison compound, removing from its various buildings every known affiliated gang member of the GFs-Mafias from the general population and reassigning them to the lockdown unit (segregation) due to their vicious gang activities. During this time, the warden had kept the gang on lockdown status for a little over a year before admitting them access back into the general population.

Well, the casualty that resulted from this rivalry has since caused the warden to place the GFs back on lockdown status, but only this time alone, with numerous of the Bloods gang members who had all been identified as having partaken in the battle. The warden had gone as far as to this time to confine all of the GFs' two members to a cell with the letters “GFs” embroidered above their cell doors. They have since been on lockdown for approximately nine months since the incident occurred. However, the prison has been nicknamed “The Shoe” for its architectural design, with its buildings being constructed in the form of a “horseshoe,” which allows the activities on the prison compound to be observed from within the buildings by the officers and the prisoners alike. Such was the case between these two rival gangs involved in the tragedy resulting from the battle between the two. Therefore, with these two gangs being observed by the inmates/officers in the buildings engaging in warfare out in the yard, there were GF members in F-building who were aware of the battle taking place. And in the same dorm, there was a young man who was about twenty-two years old and a member of the Bloods.

He had been sitting opposite the windows where the battle was observable (may his soul rest in peace), engaging in a game of dominoes, unaware of the battle being fought. And with no warnings, he was brutally attacked from behind by members of the opposing gang as he continued to play dominoes, and as a result of the numerous stab wounds he sustained, he expired before medical could even arrive to assist him. Such was the degree of his deadly wounds! The heartbreaking thing about this tragedy is that the young victim had only been at Smith State Prison for a period of only two months, with only two months remaining of his sentence before going home, but in most cases, such is the price of being affiliated with a gang.

This incident, however, has caused gang members to become more aware of rival gangs and become more protective of one another. For instance, whenever a gang member heads for the shower, there are at least two of his fellow gang members escorting him there so that while he is showering, they are posted on the outside of the shower armed with knives at the ready to attack anyone that aggressively approaches. There had also been the recent killing of a second Bloods gang member here at Smith State Prison. This senseless killing, however, resulted from the victim being caught stealing from the Mexicans. Two Mexicans cornered him off in the dorm one day, where they began to stab him repeatedly, and as a result, he also died of the attack.

Out of the prison's capacity of 1,300 inmates, you can rest assured that at least a hundred of the total have knives and are eager to use them, which is why in some prisons prison guards routinely strip-search prisoners, whereas in many others, the prison, staff couldn't care less about taking the time out to strip-search prisoners for the possessions of weapons, as long as it is prisoners killing prisoners! This is why prisoners must understand that regardless of what gang you may be affiliated with, war is not the answer and that only love can conquer hate!

Being an inmate on "death row," however, means not only having been sentenced to die but that an inmate will also no longer have physical contact of any kind with anyone except a correctional officer (denied and deprived of direct human contact). And even this contact per prison policy must be limited to only when officers have to remove an inmate from his cell rather than for medical, law library, visitation, yard call, etc.; in either event, the inmate must first be restrained completely in waist chain that binds both hands to his midsection and shackled around his ankles before the cell door opens. And because of his confinement status, he would remain in restraints throughout the duration that he is away from his cell (with the exception of recreation). And if he is fortunate enough to get visits from family, then the visitation will transpire with the inmate behind a thick, protective window while communicating through a telephone device. And it is possible that even the visits from his attorney, in some cases, could be subject to such manner. When he exits his cell for a yard call (recreation), he will exit the building for one hour while being placed inside a cage-like structure, and it is only then that the restraints are permitted to be removed outside of his cell with no exceptions. Death-row prisoners will remain live for as long as they are on death row in an eight-by-twelve cell for twenty-four hours a day (with the exception of one-hour of recreation from Monday to Friday) seven days a week. And this is, of course, the worst legal form of incarceration in the US, resulting only from a capital offense.

Inmates on death row are only granted to live until they have exhausted all their appeals. This means that there are some prisoners who have had to endure these horrific conditions for as long as twenty-plus years while seeking to be exonerated through their due process procedures (appeals). After which, if the "higher courts" fail to find grounds in their favor, which constitutes a reversal of their convictions by which they were sentenced to death row, then they would have no choice but to still face execution in the end!

There was a friend I grew up with, whom I knew attended the same school as I did, who ended up on death row. At the tender age of fifteen, he had been taken out of school and certified as an adult to be sent off to prison to serve a sentence of ten years for the crime of rape. Having entered prison as an adolescent who had obviously made a terrible mistake, he was released ten years later as a hardened criminal. And as such, within a year of his release, he had been charged with the robbery of a liquor store, which resulted in the death of the clerk on duty at the time of the robbery, who also just happened to be the owner of the establishment. He was linked to the crime and later convicted and sentenced to death row, where he has now been sitting for the past nineteen years, not successfully overcoming his appeals or having been already executed by now. I haven't a clue as to which has befallen him.

Now, as I have previously stated, at least 85 percent of the prisoners here at Smith State Prison statistically have a "life" or a "natural life" sentence. And there is one young prisoner in particular who has been sentenced to such. He was convicted for allegedly entering a convenience store that was owned by Arabs. Allegedly, he entered the store, and with the use of a firearm, he stuck up the owners thereof. There were three Arabs (may their souls rest in peace) present in the store at the time of the robbery who had all been relatives.

He demanded that they hand over their money, to which they humbly complied, and having given him their money instead of leaving the store without hurting anyone, he then shot and killed each of these individuals. He now sits in prison as a twenty-one-year-old black male, having been sentenced to "three consecutive life sentences" without the possibility of parole for what the prosecutor acknowledged as being a senseless killing of three people. And even though this crime was a capital offense punishable by death, he was spared the death penalty due to his admitting to committing the crime and the fact that he had only been seventeen years old at the time that the crime had been committed.

However, there is a second young black prisoner who was also in his teens when he committed his crime that landed him "two consecutive life sentences" and who is now twenty-two. And even a third is a young white prisoner who had been twenty-four years old when he committed his crime for which he was sentenced to a "natural life sentence" and who is currently twenty-nine years old. And it is true that one mistake can cost you everything, and these cases are a clear example of that!

There's a prisoner whose story goes like this: he, his wife, and an acquaintance while driving one day, decided that they would pull their vehicle over to the side of the road and pretend to have car trouble. Their plan was to deceive someone into believing that this had been the case while intending to rob them of their cash and valuables. The two men involved hid themselves behind the vehicle while the female with the raised hood appeared alone and vulnerable, awaiting a victim. Shortly after, there came along a married couple who, being good Samaritans, stopped to assist the seemingly stranded woman. The couple had been on their way to, of all places, a funeral when they stopped to aid the woman. The husband, who exited their truck and pulled behind it, a camper that occupied a sleeping child, approached the woman who stood near the hood of the vehicle. At that time, the two awaiting men revealed themselves. With one of them possessing a firearm, they demanded that he give over his money, which caused him to try and explain that they were on their way to a funeral and would need what little money he and his wife had, but nevertheless, he would still give some of it to them.

In cold blood, he was gunned down like a dog in the streets with his wife, witnessing the murder of her husband. She emerged from the vehicle as she ran toward his body but was also shot and killed by the gunman. The perpetrator then made his way over to the camper, and after forcing his way into it, he also murdered the sleeping child (may their souls rest in peace). All three of their bodies were later discovered in a field, with the child's body having been located in a different field than that of its parents, about two miles apart. And it was the wife of the perpetrator who eventually admitted to the authorities of having committed the horrific crime. And even though her husband, who was the gunman in all three of the murders, had strongly denied any involvement, they all were convicted, with the husband being sentenced to death. And how could anyone commit such a horrific act is beyond me, and it goes to prove that you never know just what a person may be capable of committing! This was no doubt an act of evil at its worst!

Now there are those who wholeheartedly oppose the "death penalty" while stating that "the taking of a life should be preserved for God only." The Bible states, "We are to respect the authority of the land and those that have been set in it, for they are God's advocates executing judgment upon the evildoers in the land" (1 Pet. 2:13–17). Therefore, the Bible further instructs us that "Those who live by the sword shall also perish by the sword!" In another case, there had also been a prisoner who had just met his victim through a mutual friend on the day of the incident, where the three of them hung out, drinking for the vast part of the morning, which had taken place at the mutual friend's residence.

The trail of the testimony against the perpetrator, which was later given by the mutual friend of the account of their gathering at his apartment, had been that after they had been drinking for a spell, the perpetrator had begun speaking of the three of them robbing a bank, which he suggested should take place at around noon that day.

He testified that the perpetrator had even produced the firearm that was to be used in committing the robbery that he carried on his person, a 9mm to be exact. He further testified that his friend had strongly disapproved of the robbery while stating that he "wanted nothing to do with it." He later made a phone call to his wife, asking her if she would mind coming and picking them up to give them a ride to a restaurant so that they could buy them something to eat.

Moments later after that, she arrived, and they were on their way to the restaurant. And while on their way, the perpetrator brought up again his obsession with robbing a bank, even suggesting that the victim's wife participated in the robbery by being the getaway driver in the crime. He went on to testify that as they arrived at the restaurant, he, at this point, exited the vehicle to make the purchase, leaving the three of them in the car with the perpetrator sitting in the back of the vehicle. The wife, at this point of the trial, was still in the vehicle and testified that her husband and the perpetrator had begun to argue with regard to his disapproval of the robbery and that as they both continued in their dispute, a male figure, whom her and her husband both knew, approached the passenger side of their vehicle, which was where her husband had been seated, to inquire about the commotion.

She testified that her husband informed the guy that the individual seated in the back of their vehicle had a gun on them and refused to get out of the car. It was at this point that the perpetrator went into a rage and began to yell, "Man, why did you tell this man that I have a gun held on y'all?"

She said that they had been arguing and cursing until the perpetrator asked to be let out of the vehicle, and once he had exited the car, he swiftly went around the car to the passenger side, where he began to threaten and dare him to get out of the car as she admitted that her husband had a bad temper and that with it, combined with the drinking, he exited the car. If she had known what was about to unfold, instead of waiting for their friend to return with the food, she would have driven away the second that the perpetrator had exited the car. No sooner than her husband had exited the vehicle and had taken a couple of steps toward the perpetrator did he draw a firearm and discharge it at her husband, hitting him with a fatal shot in the chest. As he was falling to the ground, he grabbed hold of the perpetrator for support, who took the butt of his pistol and hit the victim in the mouth, splitting his lip open before pushing him roughly to the ground. She and other witnesses further testified that as the victim had fallen, the perpetrator had taken his firearm and aimed the weapon at the victim's head, discharging it into the ground before kicking the victim several times in the face. His wife concluded her testimony by pointing out that as her husband, who had only been twenty-six years old, lay motionless, it was only then that the perpetrator turned and fled. She was only twenty-five years old, and they were still "newlyweds," having only been married for a period of eight months.

The perpetrator, who, prior to this murder, had just served twenty years in the federal system for bank robbery and had only been free for seven months, but for this crime, he'd been sentenced to "life plus twenty-five years for the offense of malicious murder.

Now, it's sad but true, nevertheless, that the vast majority of prisoners who have not been sentenced to death row, or even a natural life or life sentence, who still have a chance at regaining their freedom, a second chance at life, spend the majority of their prison term idly! How being incarcerated has its advantages if one chooses to utilize his time to his advantage, as well as its disadvantages of having become deprived of the ordinary privileges and rights of society. Because it's not the length of time that one serves in prison that should matter but the value of the time spent, quality time that could benefit your future!

Most prisoners do nothing more with their time than play cards dominos, watch television, and some even entertain one another about how extravagant they lived before coming to prison and of the violence that they have committed in an attempt to intimidate other inmates while not caring to utilize their time to educate themselves so that they would have a better chance at success when released. The vast majority of inmates are too busy entertaining the officers or worrying about the activities of other inmates. Nevertheless, they do not utilize their own time wisely.

They have become institutionally-minded! It is as if they have failed to grasp just how difficult it will be for them when released! Or could it be that some of them no longer care and have given up when they seem to have no expectations of life on the outside once they are released or of the opposition that awaits them, with the unemployment rates for black males already being double that of whites? They have failed to grasp the gravity of how hard it will be to reenter society as an ex-felon in terms of employment and opportunities for success. They seem not to realize that their convictions and being an ex-con only make it that much easier to be sent back to prison with a more lengthy sentence, which is why, according to the National Institute of Justice, almost 44 percent of the recently released return before the end of their first year out. But sadly, most of the younger inmates refuse to take heed of the wisdom and knowledge of the older prisoners who are among them and who try desperately to enlighten them daily about such realities. Because the end results of our mistakes in life don't have to be failures but rather positive experiences by which we obtain knowledge and wisdom!

But I can understand in part, however, why a large number of these young men of African descent may feel compelled to give up on a society that they feel has given up on them! With the eagerness of our judicious system to prosecute young men of African descent, many of whom even being first-time offenders, it's no wonder that African Americans make up an overwhelming disproportion of the US prison system. I view myself differently from most prisoners who sit around while they are on the outside. I have accepted prison as the repercussion of my mistakes and view it as a part of the game. I have been using my incarceration to my advantage! I pass away my time by studying, strategizing, and planning on how to live and maintain a productive lifestyle upon my release. A career criminal, I have been in and out of jail since the age of nineteen, all for petty crimes, of course. The federal penitentiary in Marion, Illinois, went on permanent lockdown in 1983. This created the first "control unit." Now, in addition to the federal government, some forty states have built these "maxi max" prisons.

In the state of Georgia, however, throughout the state, officials have created what is known as the Tier-2 program that began in 2013 in all of its level-five prisons. And it's just another representation of the cruel repression that grips our country today.

The Tier-2 program is a ten-month program that consists of three phases, with each phase taking three months to complete before a prisoner would go from phase 1 to phase 2.

A prisoner must elevate through the phases in the Tier-2 buildings in order to be relocated to the Tier-1 building, which is where the remaining thirty days of the ten-month period of the program is to be completed.

Some prisoners are lucky to spend this time in a single-man cell, whereas the vast majority will not but would be forced to endure the entire time spent in the Tier-2 program in an eight-by-twelve cell, 24-7 with a cellmate.

Placed outside of each cell's door is a chart mounted against the wall with the prisoner's photos, among other papers that identify the occupants of the cell, which, among the contents, is a performance sheet. This sheet is used by correctional staff to monitor the prisoner's behavior while in the tire-2 program, which is a zero-tolerance program. If a prisoner is issued a "disciplinary report," or if there is anything negative written on the "performance sheet" mentioned above, no matter how simple the accusation may be, it will result in the prisoner having to repeat whatever phase he may happen to be on at the time during his ninety-day review, which is conducted every three months. In most cases, even if a prisoner's behavior had allowed him to elevate up to the "third phase" of the Tier-2 program, he could even have his "third phase" reduced back down to "phase one" because of an accusation made against the prisoner by a correctional officer, which in most cases, be either false or highly exaggerated. It has definitely been designed to cause a prisoner to fail and, as such, for the prisoner to remain in the program when its expectations are such that a prisoner must successfully complete the ten-month program without incident (no matter how insignificant the infraction).

The Tier-2 program policy states that: "The Tier-2 Program policy establishes the criteria and guidelines for assigning offenders into the program. This program is an offender management process "and is not a punishment measure," which is the furthest from the truth! When prisoners who are in the program are deprived of TVs, radios, books, magazines, newspapers, hygiene, and canteens (such as skincare and hair products), all while being confined to an eight-by-twelve cell, twenty-three to twenty-four hours a day.

Under these adverse conditions of confinement for long periods of time (with a great deal of prisoners having already been stuck in the program for three years or better), how could anyone survive it and still remain mentally intact? There is no wonder that there have been numerous prisoners who have taken their own lives while in the Tier-2 program! Again, this program is inhumane and is a representation of the cruel repression that grips our country today. When the prisoners that are being deprived of all media outlets don't have a clue as to what is taking place in the world we live in!

These control units and super-max prisons seriously violate the rights of the prisoners that are being used to incapacitate and demoralize those held in them. Right now, there are thousands of people living in enforced solitary confinement units in US prisons, including young people in juvenile detention facilities and prisoners with mental illness.

I was retransferred back to the infamous Georgia State Prison in Reidsville, Georgia, on June 1, 2015, but two weeks prior to my transfer, while I had been still at Handcock State Prison in Sparta, Georgia, I had awakened at around 2:00 a.m. to the commotion of a horrible occurrence while being confined to admins treated segregation. My cell number, 24, was only three doors down from cell number 21, which I occupied without a cellmate, which was also the case with the occupant of cell 21. It was apparent that something was terribly wrong as it was not normal to have the warden, who was accompanied by another high-ranking official present at the prison during such a time as 2:00 a.m., and so I knew instantly that whatever the situation concerned that it had to be grave at my first glimpse of them, but what confirmed my suspicion had been the word “colonel” printed in all capital letters across the back of a T-shirt. I had awakened in time enough to witness one of the investigators snapping pictures of the scenery inside the cell with the camera being slightly tilted toward the cell’s ceiling, which pretty much told me what had occurred.

The prisoner had taken a sheet and hung himself, resulting in his death. Now, I don’t know how much time he may have been sentenced to serve in prison, but taking one’s own life only goes to show that everyone is not mentally capable of enduring long periods of time in solitary confinement. Being in a cell alone for long periods of time, such inmates would soon begin to do things like yell for hours at a time for no apparent reason, kick on the doors, and pace back and forth over the cell floor for hours while being unable to sleep or focus with incredible darkness in their spirit-beyond emotions. A deranged environment indeed! Many people in such a dark place hear voices screaming in their heads day and night, provoking suicidal thoughts and intense desires to harm themselves.

However, it wasn't until about 6:30 a.m. that the forensics and colonels had finished in ruling out foul play to have played a part in the inmate's death as they had taken the corpse down and rolled it out of the dorm to be taken to the morgue.

Since being back at Georgia State Prison, where I am now currently confined, I was informed by an officer that while conducting a count just prior to my arrival, he came across the body of an inmate who also had hung himself with him being the one to cut the inmate down. There had been yet another instance of suicidal killing that occurred at Georgia State Prison on May 21, 2016, at around 10:00 p.m., which occurred in the same dorm where I was being housed at the time at that prison as at Hancock State Prison less than a year earlier!

I don't know if God forgives people for taking their own lives, but nevertheless, may his soul rest in peace.

I've witnessed many inmates who have taken razors while confined in the solitary unit and inflicted deep wounds across mostly their wrists, arms, and with some even cutting on such areas as their necks. I've witnessed an inmate who took a razor to himself everywhere, from the top of his head to the bottom of his feet, as he was being rushed off to the medical unit one day.

There's another incident that occurred prior to my arrival back at the infamous Georgia State Prison that had also transpired in the lockdown unit that I'd like to share. Upon my entry into the K-2 dormitory, which is where I had been assigned to live, I quickly noticed that the door of cell number 22 to my left was secured with yellow crime scene tape that had been bound across the door with it being shut. I didn't quite know exactly what to make out of it at first sight but soon learned the cause of it when I overheard a lieutenant speaking of what had occurred a week prior to my arrival.

It was said that a prisoner who had a visit during that time had smuggled narcotics back to his cell, which was brought into the prison by his visitors. His visitors just happened to be his mother and girlfriend, with the mother, of all people, being the one who had smuggled drugs into the prison at the request of her son. The methamphetamine, however, had been placed inside several balloons that he'd swallowed in his way of smuggling the drugs back to his cell. But shortly after he had arrived back at his cell, it was then that he began to bang on the cell door while yelling for the attention of an officer to inform him/her of what he had done! It turned out the balloons that contained the narcotics he had swallowed had either somehow punctured or become untied inside of him, which he obviously realized was the cause of him feeling intoxicated before having a chance to defecate as a means of regaining access to the narcotics.

Having gained the attention of the officers, he quickly informed them of what he had done and were immediately escorted to the prison medical ward, but as fate would have it, there was simply nothing much to be done by them that could save this prisoner's life, and as a result, he expired shortly after his arrival onto the medical ward from a drug overdose. Sadly, you have prisoners who lose their lives for all sorts of reasons while incarcerated, whether it's in actual prison or in the city or county jails.

Like there was once in the Dekalb County jail in Decatur, Georgia, which consists of two ten-story twin towers, which were constructed to accommodate the capacity of 3,500 men. There was an inmate who was at the time being confined on the tenth floor of the jail who had taken sheets and tied them each to the other, which he'd used in an attempt to escape the jail by lowering himself from the window of his cell to the city street below. No sooner had he begun his descent the knot in the sheet slipped apart, causing him to fall the remaining eight or nine stories to his death. However, prison is a place that most prisoners have come to term as being "the modern-day plantation."

For instance, at Georgia State Prison where I've observed as part of the prisoners' compound, a "factory" of some sort where Monday through Friday inmates are sent to perform work duties. And also, during my confinement at Smith State Prison in Glennville, Georgia, I've also observed that they have a "tag plant" in operation where a couple of busloads of prisoners would be taken to print automobile license places. And while at Hancock State Prison in Sparta, Georgia, I could vividly see from the window of my cell a third factory where numerous prisoners were enticed to work while not being allowed to earn a single cent for their Monday to Friday, eight-to-twelve-hours-a-day labor. I have seen as many as four tractor-trailers at once, all waiting to be loaded at these prison factories with prison-manufactured products to be transported back to the "free world" for profit as a result of the prisoners' free labor.

In fact, prison is the only legalized place in America where people can work without pay! And in most prisons, they are not! Yet I would observe the regular eighteen-wheelers from the "free world" that would pull up to the loading docks of these prison factories and transport the goods manufactured by the prisoners to society for profit! And then you have literally right across the street from Georgia State Prison, Roger State Prison, which is where the prisoners harvest all the food produced from the fields that feed the prisoners throughout the state, which even has its own "dairy." On the sides of each of its milk cartons is written "Rogers State Prison Dairy, A Division of Food and Farm Services, Georgia Correctional Industries, Reidsville, Georgia 30453." Apart from these factories, prisoners are also being used to perform every other manual labor necessary to the upkeep and function of the State Department of Corrections. Jobs that had not been for the manpower and the free labor of the prisoners who, in most cases, are eager to perform them out of ignorance. Then, the State Department of Corrections would have no choice but to employ professionals to come into these institutions to perform them. These are duties that would have cost the institutions millions of dollars annually! This is why slavery was seen as acceptable based on skin color. Now, slavery is socially acceptable, but it happens every day.

The State and Federal Constitutions still allow involuntary servitude (slavery), though most people are unaware of this fact! If it had not been for the ignorance of the prisoners who are willing to maintain free of charge the very prisons in which they are being confined for many years, despite the fact that at the duration of their sentences, they would only be given by the State Department of Corrections twenty-five dollars ($25) regardless of their many years of labor or the fact that they may have nothing to return to upon release after so many years behind bars. And a twenty-five-dollar check at the duration of their sentence, you can bet, won't go very far! Nevertheless, most inmates would embrace the opportunity to be used in this capacity while not caring to have utilized their time to benefit them.

There have been many instances when an inmate refused to show up to perform his assigned details, and he would be issued a "disciplinary report," which would result in sanctions being taken against the inmate. There are two crews. An a.m. and a p.m. crew. Two busloads per crew. When the buses carry the morning shift in at noon, they then transfer back to the evening shift to the workplace, where they will labor sometimes until dusk. And it is like the inmates are waiting in line to work for free as opposed to doing something with their time that could benefit them upon release. They seem to fail to realize that being an ex-convict faced with real-world choices for the first time in years, transitioning can be jarring, and it doesn't take much for a prisoner, who is handed only $25 upon release, to wind up behind bars again.

Prison, which is claimed to be a place of correction for the men and women who have made a mistake and find themselves there, is, in reality, a business that extorts the prisoners for the benefit of the institutions. As such, it attracts its employees straight out of high school. Out of the abundance of wealth that prisoners are making and saving the system, it seems only fair that they should be giving back at least $15 to $20 per week, which would allow the unfortunate ones to purchase commissary (store items). But it only goes to show that rather than give these men and women something back for their many years of devoted servitude; it is because of the Jim Crow laws of the Thirteenth Amendment, passed by Congress on January 31, 1865. Ratified on December 6, 1865, that the system would rather slave them instead.

Note: A portion of Article IV, section 2 of the Constitution was superseded by the Thirteenth Amendment. Section 1. "Neither slavery nor involuntary servitude (except as a punishment for crime whereof the party shall have been duly convicted shall exist within the United States, or any place subjected to their jurisdiction." Clearly, the US Constitution did not abolish slavery; it simply transferred it into the prison system. There was a speech delivered by a white slave owner named Williams Lynch (better known as the "Willie Lynch" speech) on the bank of the James River in 1712 in Virginia. His speech surrounded what he recognized to be his "fool-proof method for controlling black slaves, that if installed correctly, it would control the slaves for at least 300 years to come if not thousands." And sadly, this system, to some degree, still holds true today, more or less due to the ignorance of our own race in one form or another. People say that the criminal justice system doesn't work. But I've come to believe that it works perfectly, just as slavery did, as a matter of economic and political policy. Considering the fact that slavery is legalized in prison today by the Thirteenth Amendment of the US Constitution.

Now you have all sorts of characters in prison; speaking of which, there is one such inmate who was confined to administrative segregation, where prisoners are locked down twenty-three to twenty-four hours per day. These inmates, for different reasons, would oftentimes eject their body waste out from behind their secured cell doors to on-duty officers and even other prisoners. The consequences they would face for this animal-like behavior would normally range anywhere from being hit with a "free world" charge, a disciplinary report, and being placed in a seventy-two-hour strip cell with occasional physical retaliation by prison officials. But the inmate whom I'm referring to was the first that I'd witnessed to have free world charges brought against him. And the inmate, prior to the charges being brought, had committed this act numerous times. He was eventually warned by the warden that if he ever did it again, he would bring free-world charges against him. Failing to take heed to the warning, the prisoner was eventually taken momentarily from the prison down to the county's district attorney's office, where he was fingerprinted and charged with two counts of "aggravated assault" and two counts of "destructing the duties of a correctional officer."

The inmate has been in prison serving a ten-year sentence and only had three months remaining before maxing out on the sentence now upon the duration of his initial sentence and must be expedited to the county jail here in Reidsville, Georgia, to face these new charges. These long-term periods of isolation, however, have the tendency to dehumanize most prisoners. Black Panther Party Member Angela Davis (1975) stated, "Jails and prisons are designed to break human beings, to convert the population into specimens in a zoo-obedient to our keepers but dangerous to each other." It's not unusual, however, to learn of prisoners who have been sentenced to serve a set sentence, after which they would have to be released. They have accumulated more time for themselves than that which was initially sentenced to prison for them to serve for such things as violence, drugs, etc., while incarcerated.

For instance, there was one prisoner who, after being sentenced to five years in prison, had taken the lives of two fellow cons while in prison. During sentencing at his trial for these killings, he was sentenced to two consecutive life sentences. At this time, he attempted to remove the weapon (firearm) of one of the courtroom deputies and was shot and killed in the act by a second officer who was also on security duty in court. Prison by no means guarantees positive changes! Some may even argue that it makes people worse! The vast majority of prison guards employed by the Department of Corrections are females. For instance, there are at least eight female employees to every male employee employed at Georgia State Prison in Reidsville, Georgia. And the vast majority of prisoners who have been incarcerated for a substantial amount of time with sentences ranging from ten years to life have pushed many self-respecting, rational-thinking, decent-minded men to a quest for excitement (acts of desperation).

So most prisoners, as a result of most states forbidding prisoners the physical intimacy of a woman (with the state of Georgia being one that does), have become exhibitionists. Certain prisons even forbid a married prisoner from having any type of sexual relations with his wife, regardless of the length of his sentence to be served in prison. The only physical contact permitted between married couples would be a casual embrace upon their arrival and a similar one during the duration of the visit. Nevertheless, there are many prisoners who are not married, and as a result of the long-term deprivation of the physical affection of a woman, have become extremely overpowered by their lust for a woman! Having become exhibitionists, prisoners would stand in plain view of any female personnel such as nurses, doctors, counselors, etc., and masturbate—a frequent occurrence in any correctional institution by prisoners. And as such, it helps to minimize the possibility of rape among inmates, which rarely occurs. Some females would process a "disciplinary report," nevertheless, against an inmate's behavior, whereas the vast majority of them would simply welcome an inmate's actions as a moment of pleasure.

States like Georgia still honor the Jim Crow laws and, therefore, know that to permit a black man (because we are and have always been the target) to indulge in female relations while incarcerated defeats the purpose of the "design" to commit genocide against the black race. Clearly, the system is and has always been designed to victimize African Americans in this country, which the statistics have proven time and time again. Now, if I haven't shared anything with you this far, that would discourage you from any illegal activities that may lead you to prison. Then, if you love to indulge in "good food," don't come to prison! As the old saying goes, "The grass is truly greener on the other side of the fence!" If the food isn't bad enough and is of low quality, then what of those are prepared and served by the prisoners themselves? You may want to consider that on top of this, the State Department of Corrections (at the time of my writing this book) doesn't feed its prisoners lunch on weekends, which include Friday, Saturday, and Sunday. And neither on holidays! When holidays happen to fall on a Thursday, which they often do, prisoners would have to endure four straight days on only two meals with no extra provided to supplement the lunch—meals that are served even a toddler can devour. Just enough of the same ole, tasteless, no variety, every day, recycled meals to keep the prisoners from starving to death! Prison!

Any federal or state penal institution that incarcerates prisoners accused of, convicted of, and sentenced for the violation of criminal law (insufficient food, insufficient education, rehabilitation, cruel and unusual punishment, abuse, and excessive force are all common issues that prisoners are forced to endure in the American prison system). A world that consists of razor wire, gun towers, and concrete walls! A gigantic human warehouse! A miserable place of captivity! And a place I wouldn't wish upon my worst enemy!

# PART 3

## Is Our justice System Biased?

As the contemporary examination of the impact of mass incarceration on black communities continues, it is important that we remember the wisdom of the Black Panther Party and understand the significance of having access to the most basic element of justice in the United States: access to a fair trial. Being in prison, one of my ambitions has been the struggle as a pro se petitioner to try and get myself back in court (without the aid of an attorney) through what is known as a "Habeas Corpus Petition.

While seeking relief on the grounds that my state-appointed attorney representation had been ineffective, having succeeded in obtaining a day in court to be heard on the petition, I was transferred momentarily to Reidsville, Georgia, which is where the court session had been arranged to take place.

Upon my arrival, I was momentarily placed inside a holding cell in prison, and it just so happened that during the time that I had been taken to court, it was on what is known as a "transfer day." This means, of course, that there are two days per week, Tuesday and Thursday, that the Georgia Department of Corrections relocates its prisoners throughout the state. This would also include some of the prisoners who are in the city and county jails who have been convicted and, as such, have received a prison sentence. The prisoners that are in the jails throughout the state at this time are either picked up by state officials or delivered to the state facilities by means of the Sheriff's Department, which brings me to the point I intend to make. Having momentarily been placed into one of the prison holding cells, I swiftly acknowledged that of the prisoners that had been delivered from the nearby jails who had also been placed inside the same holding cell as I, which consisted of about fifty men totally that occupied the cell. I was able to identify them by the civilian clothes that they wore as opposed to the prison stripes that official prisoners, such as myself, wore. I began to count them, and in the process of doing so, I quickly realized that there had been twenty-two of them that had come from the jails. But what I found disturbing about my observation was the fact that out of the twenty-two prisoners that were sent from the nearby jails, one had been white, another was Mexican, and the remaining twenty of them were black! A discrepancy indeed!

And another I found astounding was the fact that I alone appeared to be the only black prisoner in the cell out of approximately forty other blacks who weren't oblivious to the matter. This serves to show that whites and African Americans live in completely different worlds when it comes to race and the criminal justice system. There are so many more African Americans than whites in our prisons, and it penalizes African Americans at almost every juncture in the criminal justice system, according to The Report of the National Criminal Justice Commission. More than a third of the young African-American men aged eighteen to thirty-four in some of our major cities are either in prison or under some form of criminal justice supervision. And there are many issues of race and crime that affect other racial and ethnic minorities, not just African-Americans. I focus primarily on African Americans because we are our largest minority group, and we have the highest rates of imprisonment.

The United States imprisons African-American men at a rate six times that of white men, with African-American males making up less than 7 percent of the US population, yet we comprise almost half of the prison and jail population. Almost three out of four prison admissions today are either African-American or Hispanic, and 90 percent of the prison admissions for drug offenses are African American or Hispanic. And if the percentage of African minorities in prison continues to increase at the same rate, almost two out of three of all young African-American men nationwide between the ages of eighteen and thirty-four will be in prison by the year 2021.

There are seven African Americans, each white, in prison. This evidence strongly suggests that as African Americans work through the system from arrest to punishment, we encounter harsher treatment than whites. This is not to say the system is never fair to African Americans, but that the statistics indicate that African Americans, as a class of offenders, receive harsher treatment than whites. This fact has been borne out by studies that show whites are released more often before trial, pay less money to bail themselves out of jail, and receive significantly better deals in plea bargaining than minorities. Is there a racial bias? Well, the first place where racial disparities are usually measured is at the point of arrest. Most studies reveal that most police officers will casually admit that race is used as a factor when the police decide to follow, detain, search, or arrest. Once they make an arrest, police usually refer the case to a prosecutor, who decides whether to press charges or dismiss the matter. The majority of available studies conclude that racial discrimination can and often does play a role in prosecutorial decisions. The study found that crimes involving white victims and African-American offenders were much more likely to be upgraded in severity by the prosecutor, while crimes involving African-American victims and white offenders were more likely to be downgraded. The reason why an upgraded case leads to more serious charges, a more energized prosecution, and higher sentences, but again, this pattern does not necessarily hold true in all jurisdictions at all times.

A study by the Hartford Courant of 150,000 criminal cases in Connecticut found that an African-American or Hispanic man must pay, on average, double the bail of a white man for the same offense. In drug cases, the study found that the average bond for African-Americans and Hispanics in several areas of the state was four times higher than the bond for whites. The racial disparities in bail prompted the chief court administrator in Connecticut to charge publicly that judges use excessive bonds to punish minorities who had not been convicted. And it makes you wonder, what happened to the presumption of being innocent until proven guilty?

A similar study in Florida, conducted for the State Department of Corrections, found strong evidence of racial bias in the treatment of African-American defendants before trial. The sample of almost three thousand adult offenders showed that being African American significantly increased the likelihood of incarceration before trial. More than 90 percent of criminal cases where the defendant faces a prison sentence ended in a "deal" in which the defendant pleads guilty to a lesser charge rather than face the risk of trial and a longer sentence. During negotiations between defense attorneys and prosecutors—the plea-bargaining process—prosecutors have wide discretion to be tough on some and more generous with others. Evidence suggests it is minorities who get the worst deals. A comprehensive study of racial bias in plea bargaining was carried out in California by the San Jose Mercury News in 1991. A computer analysis of almost seven hundred thousand criminal cases in California from 1990 demonstrated that at virtually every stage of pretrial plea-bargaining, whites were more successful than minorities.

All else being equal, whites did better than African Americans and Hispanics, getting cases dropped dismissed, avoiding harsher extra charges, and having their criminal records wiped clean. For instance, here's Aaron's story:

My name is Aaron, and the crime resulting in my confinement is reckless driving and manslaughter, which occurred in 2001. I'm a family man who is married to my beautiful wife of thirty-six years. My wife and I share three adult sons and a daughter. I was twenty-three years old at the time that we married and forty-seven at the time of the tragedy that changed my life forever. I am currently fifty-nine years old as I sit here in prison today, reflecting back on this horrific chapter of my life.

I had been a professional truck driver for a little over twenty years prior to the incident that landed me in prison. I've driven nationwide for fifteen of those years without ever receiving as much as a traffic ticket. But as fate would have it, I had driven from Jacksonville, Florida, to Georgia one day, and as I was traveling along the interstate, it began to drizzle for about fifteen minutes, which slowly increased the further I drove. I continued traveling along the interstate at a decreased speed of about forty-five miles per hour when, out of nowhere, a traffic jam, which, due to the constant rainfall, caught me off guard. Desperately, I began to try to break the momentum of the truck, but to no avail! It all happened so suddenly.

The next thing I knew, there I was, living in this horrifying nightmare that unfolded right before my very eyes. The eighty-five-thousand-pound load that the truck was carrying, with the exception of the weight of the truck, smashed into the rear of the immediate vehicle, causing my heart to fall into my stomach. This, of course, caused a chain reaction whose impact resulted in the destruction of eight vehicles and, worst of all, the unfortunate death of four people! I didn't drink alcohol or use drugs at the time of the incident, and neither do I now! In fact, I was given a breathalyzer test within fifteen minutes of the accident, and the results were negative. The four casualties had all been white females, one of which was a child.

On the other hand, I was a black male who had no prior criminal record, was a family man, and had twenty years of truck-driving experience on a professional level prior to the incident. But none of it seemed to matter because I was arrested in spite of the negative results of the breathalyzer and later convicted of reckless driving and manslaughter and sentenced to thirty-five years in prison on what should have been ruled accidental! Nevertheless, my heart continues to grieve for the victims and go out to their families daily! I am so sorry that they had to lose their lives in this unfortunate tragedy, and I would give anything if I could reverse it! However, there is a white prisoner whom I overheard sharing a similar story as my own as to what led him to prison one day while we were part of a prison program called Motivation for Change.

He shared that he had been among family and friends on the day of the incident that led him to prison, drinking and having a good time. Sometime afterward, he decided to leave with the intention of driving to a nearby state to visit his grandparents. But being in his condition, several of his family members and friends discouraged him from getting behind the wheel until alcohol had worn off. He insisted that he was fine, disregarding their concerns as he entered his vehicle to make the trip to visit his grandparents in a nearby state. He went on to share, however, that after he had been driving for maybe an hour or so, it also began to rain, and before he knew it, he found himself in an accident that claimed the lives of a young mother and her daughter. He was given a breathalyzer test, which had proven to be way beyond the legal limits. He was charged with vehicle homicide, which was later reduced to manslaughter by the district attorney, and allowed to accept a plea-bargaining deal, resulting in a ten-year sentence with only two of which to be served in prison, with the remaining eight being placed on probation.

He had also been provided with an opportunity as a part of his plea deal that once he'd finished serving the two years, he would then be allowed to enter into a rehabilitation program and that upon successfully completing the program, he would have his "manslaughter charge expunged from his record." He would no longer have his eight-year probation, and his criminal record would be wiped clean! Nothing left to indicate that he had ever caused the deaths of a young mother and her daughter while driving under the influence of alcohol! And the sad reality of it is that both of his victims had been black, whereas the victims involved in my case had been white! So maybe you shouldn't drive "black" as opposed to "drunk" in Georgia! He went on to share that the reason why the district attorney had decided to make him such a deal was because he had only been nineteen at the time with no prior criminal record. But the real reason behind the DA's deal, which he failed to admit, though it was written all over his face, was that he was white and his victims were black! I mean, when you consider the overwhelming number of young African-American men who were of the same age or younger when committing their crimes and had also been first-time offenders with "no" criminal history yet had been sentenced to anywhere from fifteen to twenty years in prison for crimes that neither involved taking a life.

For example, there is one such case involving a young black man who has confided in me that he was eighteen years old when he committed his crime and twenty-three at the time that I met him. He shared with me that he was a first-time offender as well who had never been convicted of a crime prior to the offense of theft by taking. Entering an auto and taking a few possessions of the car owner that was left in the vehicle for which he was sentenced to serve ten years in prison for a crime that was in no way violent, nor did it involve the taking of a life! Among the findings of the California study, however, of 71,668 adults who had no prior record and were charged with a felony, one-third of whites had their charges reduced to a misdemeanor or less. Only a quarter of African Americans and Hispanics received such reductions.

Because of tougher plea-bargaining deals, convictions for the sale of drugs sent Hispanics to state prison (as opposed to county jail or probation) at twice the rate of whites. African Americans were sent to state prison at rates one-third higher than whites. White first-time offenders were placed in community-based rehabilitation programs instead of prison at almost twice the rate of Hispanics and African-Americans. Some of the cruelest form of racial discrimination in the area of sentencing takes place in the application of the death penalty. The most comprehensive study of the death penalty found that killers of whites were eleven times more likely to be condemned to death than killers of African-Americans.

Discrimination in the application of the death penalty can be seen most vividly by focusing on the race of the victim. Prosecutors nationwide—more than nine out of ten of whom are white—tend to seek the death penalty more often if the victim is white. To take one typical example, Georgia prosecutors sought the death penalty in 70 percent of the cases where the perpetrator was African-American and the victim was white. When there was a white killer and an African-American victim, the same prosecutors sought the death penalty in only 15 percent of the cases. The Harvard Law Review published in 1988 a comprehensive legal dissection of racial discrimination in the criminal justice system. It is the overall conclusion of this authoritative journal that is so persuasive: After looking at every component of the criminal justice system, it determined that there is evidence that discrimination exists against African Americans at almost every stage of the criminal justice process.

Other researchers across the political spectrum have reached the same conclusion. A 1994 study of race bias led by researcher Robert Crutchfield concluded that a "growing body of evidence suggests that justice is by no means guaranteed" for minorities in the criminal justice system. Research by criminologists Alfred Blumstein and Joan Petersilia compared arrests to rates of incarceration and concluded that a significant portion of the racial disparities in prison is accounted for by racial discrimination. And although this is most certainly a form of genocide, most people do not understand the political uses of prisons in this way. According to commission member Norval Morris, there is "measurable racial discrimination in our police practices, in our prosecutorial practices, and in our sentencing." Morris concluded that the whole law and order movement that we have heard so much about is, in operation though not in intent, anti-black and anti-underclass—not in plan, not in desire, not in intent, but in operation."

Several studies link involvement in the criminal justice system with lowered employment prospects. Employers tend to pass over applications that have a criminal record of any kind—even if the record only reflects an arrest for a minor infraction and even if that arrest is unfound. Andrew Shapiro found that about four million Americans have lost their right to vote because of a criminal conviction. A disproportionate number are African-American. Sadly, many laws that took away the right to vote were passed in the early part of the century with the express purpose of undermining the political power of African Americans.

In Virginia, a legislator explained that the criminal disenfranchisement law was passed with a view to the elimination of every Negro voter. In Louisiana in 1898, the chief justice of the Supreme Court urged that the law be passed to establish the supremacy of the white race. And what is ironic is that it is contemporary criminal justice policies that are, to some degree, making the wishes of segregationist legislators from the early part of the century come true, and as a result of such policies, about five million Americans have lost their right to vote with a significant disproportionate being black because of a criminal conviction. The disenfranchisement laws were designed and originated over a century ago, but due to the contemporary criminal justice policies of the twenty-first century, they have made the wishes of segregationist legislators of the early part of the century come true.

In the 2008 and 2012 elections, votes from African Americans represented about 13 percent of the overall total nationally, according to the Washington-based Joint Center for Political and Economic Studies. It is through voting that we as a nation have the ability to affect change in the democratic process, providing, however, that the right officials are elected. Because if the majority of African-Americans cannot vote, then we have limited power to elect certain government officials who get to run our cities, counties, states, and the country! And in the prison system, many prisoners cannot read or write properly, and most do not know the law. And being indigent, this leaves them helpless to defend themselves against a devious and corrupt court system.

Obama's "Health Care Act" was to assure affordable health care to every unfortunate citizen who didn't have it and couldn't afford it. This policy was designed to assure them the "insurance policy" that they wouldn't have been able to afford otherwise. But President Obama had been criticized by the Republican Party for every decision he brought on behalf of the American people like no president before him. When you consider that there are approximately fifty million citizens who are living below the poverty line in this country, must we forget about them? Is it not the proper function of every person to live and not merely exist? Then what kind of nation do we have that wouldn't want to support its commander-in-chief in the health, growth, and development of its citizens?

Obama, an intellectual and fluent-speaking black president whom the Republican Party conspired to see failure, while in return failing to consider the well-being of the citizens over race! They must have forgotten that the government's first priority should be the basic needs of its citizens—food, health care, shelter employment, education, and livable incomes for all Americans beyond race. The government's concerns should be directly addressed to its people regarding various aspects of America's public policies that affect the quality of life and economic well-being of all Americans. Such behavior of our elected officials doesn't only seem incomprehensible but entirely insensitive to the welfare of every man, woman, and child in America. This is proof that we have members in Congress and in the Supreme Court today who are not in the least bit sympathetic or enthusiastic about the principles of fairness! With so many of them in authority not doing the right thing, but rather holding on to power. And we must vote them out!

Governments are instituted among Men, deriving their just Powers from the Consent of the Governed, that whenever any Form of Government becomes destructive of these Ends, it is the Right of the People to alter or to abolish it, and to institute new Government…it is their Right, it is their Duty, to throw off such Government, and to provide new Guards for their future security. (Thomas Jefferson, "The Declaration of Independence")

A government for the people, by the people, and of the people! America, however, has proven consistently that it is an enemy of the African race. So this should come as no surprise. For it is because of poverty and a lack of education that young men and women commit crimes while ignorant of the harsh reality that awaits them in an unjust system. So, we must teach them that in spite of their struggles to survive, there are better ways. The goal of the government is to create two societies: one civilian and the other an institutional society. The famous 1968 Kerner report had warned that America was in danger of becoming "two societies...separate and unequal." As much as I would like to believe that this nation does indeed offer African Americans equal opportunities for life, liberty, and the pursuit of happiness, this is why, as black men, we need to step up to the plate and become fathers to our children! One who will teach his child to develop structure, a solid foundation, and standards that they refuse to negotiate in their lives. Any teenage male can perhaps become a dad, but it takes a man who would protect, provide, and foster a child to be a father! And know that God will hold man "accountable" whom he has ordained head of the household for the proper upbringing of his children!

Yes, we as men will be held accountable to the Lord for "spiritual leadership!" See 1 Peter 3:5–6 and Proverb 22:6. So, brothers, let's not forget that there is much more to having a child than just the sexual intercourse of it! Seeing how most brothers appear to think that once they have donated their sperm, their involvement is completed, when in fact, it has just begun, but because many men have found it easier to just walk away rather than to face up to their responsibilities as fathers, it is the main reason why there are so many young black men in prison today!

Too many kids today are growing up without a father's influence. And with many African-American men being ignorant to the true value of the woman, that she is God's gift to man, they begin to view her as nothing more than a "sex object" to be filled with children and then abandon. They abandon not only the woman but their children as well, having failed to acknowledge her as his queen and soulmate and his children as his flesh and blood, whose responsibility is to guide and protect; he neglects and abandons them both. Yes, they need parents who express unconditional love for them. Show them why you love their mother. When they see you loving their mother, treating her like a queen, and giving her consideration and honor, they'll admire, appreciate, and emulate their awesome father! So, is there a racial bias? Well, as these studies have demonstrated, there most certainly has been strong evidence of racial bias in the treatment of African-American defendants in the criminal justice system. And I truly believe that as "iron sharpens iron," whenever we have been given an opportunity to point out an issue, to educate

others, and to open their eyes, then we should.

# PART 4

## Though They're Gone, They're Not Forgotten

The difficulties and struggles of today are but the price we must pay for the accomplishments and victories of tomorrow.

—Williams J. H. Boetcker

Hate is too great a burden to bear. It injures the hater more than it injures the hated.

—Coretta Scott King

Prison is filled with African-American men who have been incarcerated since the early age of sixteen, many of whom are in their mid-twenties. And the thing that disturbs me the most with regard to most of these young men is the numerous senseless black-on-black attacks and the lack of unity among them. With the rate of death in this country, from homicide being six times higher for black males than that for whites, it's as if we don't love ourselves when all other nationalities appear to cherish members of their race.

If one is hungry, then the other provides bread. Many legends and pioneers have laid down their lives to pave the way for us today, and is this how we show our gratitude? Then we must rid ourselves of the "every man for himself" way of thinking and learn to pull together instead! Today, I overheard a sixty-one-year-old lieutenant here at the prison trying to speak a word of knowledge to a young black prisoner who appeared to be in his early twenties. All of a sudden, the young man rudely yelled out, "F—— Martin Luther King! We're still locked up!"

At this point, the lieutenant asked the prisoner, "But why are you locked up?"

He refused to answer but instead repeated, "F—— Martin Luther King! We're still locked up!" He yelled for the second time. Not only did this not show any respect toward the deceased, but to boldly disrespect the life and legacy of a true pioneer as the late Dr. King in such a way is simply just another example of the ignorance of many young black men.

There was another prisoner who I asked today, "Do you know where Dr. Martin Luther King Jr. was assassinated?"

"In a house," the young prisoner replied.

And after taking a moment to see if he was, in fact, serious and realizing that he was, I then began to share with him that Dr. King (may his soul rest in peace) was assassinated on April 4, 1968, for his patriotic role in the civil rights movement in Memphis, Tennessee, while standing among a group of his associates on a motel balcony. In what turned out to be the last speech that he delivered on the evening of April 3, 1968, Dr. King stated, "I've been cautioned not to come back to Memphis. Like anybody, I would like to live a long life. Longevity has its place. But I'm not concerned about that now. I just want to do God's will." He knew, and, without fear, was willing and prepared to face death head on to do God's will! How brave was that! And he did it all for the equal rights of all men!

At precisely a minute past 6:00 p.m. on the evening of April 4, 1968, Dr. King, among a group of his staff, had exited the Lorraine Motel to go out for dinner when he was shot through the jaw by a single bullet of a sniper, which exited the side of his neck. He was pronounced dead in less than two hours in the emergency operating room at Memphis's St. Joseph's Hospital. Dr. Martin Luther King Jr. preached on a Sunday morning in 1957; he fought the temptation to retaliate against a society steeped in racism.

"How do you go about loving your enemies?" he asked the Dexter Avenue Baptist congregation in Montgomery, Alabama.

"Begin with yourself… When the opportunity presents itself for you to defeat your enemy, that is the time that you must not do it." Quoting from the words of Jesus, King said, "Love your enemies, bless them that curse you, do good to them that hate you, and pray for them that despitefully use you…; that ye may be the children of your Father which is in heaven" (Matt. 5:44–45.) Dr. Martin Luther King Jr. dedicated his life to the love and justice of all human beings, and for that, he died with more than sixty thousand people who had gathered at the Ebenezer Baptist Church on the day of his funeral to pay their respects.

I went on to share with him that I once lived in Memphis, Tennessee, from 1994 to 1995, during which time I had the honor of visiting the very motel where he had been assassinated. I explained to him that even though it had been twenty-six years since his assassination at the time, the Lorraine Motel still existed but only as a tourist site. As such, the very vehicles that they had driven on that day had still been parked outside the establishment. The vehicles were two late-model black Cadillacs with white leather interiors and ten white-wall tires. The upkeeping of the vehicles was superb! Twenty-six years later, they had looked as if they had just been manufactured. And up on what I believe to have been the third balcony, there was a yellow police ribbon that surrounded the exact location in front of a motel room door where Dr. King had been assassinated.

I found it hard to believe that after all those years, there I was, standing in such a sad part of our culture's history. And although it was an honorable experience, it still served as a reminder of all the tragedy and misery which our history is full of! Speaking of which, I am reminded of other horrific occurrences, such as that of Medgar Evers, a black civil rights activist (may his soul rest in peace) who was returning home from an NAACP meeting in Jackson, Mississippi, when he had been shot through the back and killed outside his front door by a sniper's bullet in 1963. And that of Sammy Younge Jr., who on January 3, 1965, was shot in the back of the head outside a Standard Oil gas station in Tuskegee, Alabama, for trying to use a "white only" restroom (may his soul rest in peace). He had been a twenty-one-year-old SCCN student and a veteran just out of the Navy. Fresh out of the military from serving his country, he had been shot down like a dog in the streets for something as simple as using the toilet by a white supremacist. He had been pursued out of the establishment by the clerk, who was a sixty-nine-year-old white male with a firearm. And although Sammy had been shot and killed in public in cold blood in broad daylight, at trial, the perpetrator was found not guilty.

Sammy had asked to use the clerk, who would allow him access to the "outside restroom" located around the side of the establishment. And upon accepting the keys and reaching the restroom, Sammy discovered what he had already expected. The restroom was filthy; the sink had been stuck up, and there was no toilet paper in the restroom. Refusing to use the restroom in its condition, Sammy reentered the establishment and confronted the clerk to tell him about its condition. After this, he requested to use the inside restroom, which had been reserved for whites only. And after being denied access by the clerk, Sammy began to mention the Supreme Court ruling, which did away with segregation in all public businesses (known as the Jim Crow law), and therefore, he had a right to use the inside restroom.

The clerk becomes angry at Sammy's remarks about the Supreme Court's rulings, so he retrieves a firearm from beneath the counter and orders Sammy to leave the establishment. Sammy, who disregarded any further attempts to use the "white only" restroom, humbly exited the establishment, only to realize that he was being pursued by the clerk who still carried the firearm. Being that the Greyhound bus station was located across the street from the gas station where Sammy's vehicle had still been parked, Sammy, with the clerk in pursuit of him, thought it best not to reenter his vehicle but instead headed toward the crowded station to minimize the chances of the clerk discharging the firearm in public for the fear of witnesses. And this rationale of Sammy had been reasonable given the circumstances he faced, but nevertheless, with the perpetrator having no regard for the safety of others or fearing potential witnesses, he pursued Sammy across the street, where he discharged the firearm into the back of the young man's head in a public business in broad daylight. But in the trial by an all-white jury, he was found not guilty!

And then you have the brutal murder of Emmett Till, a fourteen-year-old boy from Chicago, Illinois (may his soul rest in peace), who in August of 1954 was spending the summer with relatives in Mississippi when his body had been later pulled from the bottom of the Tallahatchie River. He had been shot through the head with one of his eyes plucked out and a seventy-five-pound cotton gin fan wired around his neck. He had been witnessed being dragged out of bed by two white men on the night he was killed for allegedly saying "Bye, baby" to a white woman while leaving a country store.

One of the killers explained to a magazine writer, "What else could I do? He thought he was as good as any white man." The two men, with one being the white woman's husband, by an all-white jury, were found not guilty of Emmett Till's murder despite the testimony of a black witness who had the courage to put his own life on the line by stepping forward and testifying.

And how can I possibly forget about the four little girls who were killed at the Sixteenth Street Baptist Church in Birmingham, Alabama, on the morning of September 15, 1963, from a bomb explosion that ended their young lives? The church was celebrating its annual youth day, having the building filled with children when an explosion occurred. After the smoke had settled, there had been twenty-one children were injured, and four killed on a Sunday morning in God's house!

Neither can I forget about the marchers who attempted their march from Selma to Montgomery over a fifty-mile journey when they were attacked on the Edmund Pettus Bridge and beaten by state troopers on March 7, 1965. A six-hundred-person civil rights demonstration ended in violence when the day's events became known as "Bloody Sunday."

In a small town called Poplarville, Mississippi, there was a young black man by the name of Mack Charles Parker who, in 1955, had been accused of rape, and before his trial could even begin, Parker was dragged out of jail by a lynch mob and shot to death; his body had been dumped in a river, and no one was ever indicted for his murder, although he had been dragged out of jail by the lynch mob. The Supreme Court ruling in 1946 made segregation illegal (a federal law) on interstate buses. Mrs. Rosa Parks (may her soul rest in peace) had been arrested for refusing to give up her seat to a white man in Montgomery, Alabama, on December 1, 1955, and nine years after that, the Supreme Court ruling had outlawed segregation on interstate buses. And it's sad, however, to learn of the type of violence that was inflicted upon those who protested in a nonviolent movement for civil rights, such as endured upon those during the "sit-ins," "freedom rides," and "Mississippi summer."

These protests were being made in an attempt to get the federal government to respond to its own laws put in effect in ways that it had not from the beginning. This means, what good is it to pass a law if you're not going to stand by it? And just in case some of you may not be familiar with the "sit-ins," "freedom rides," and Mississippi summer," then allow me to put some insight into these terms.

The "sit-ins" all begin with a group of Southern SCCN college students who would enter segregated businesses during the civil rights movement that wouldn't allow blacks to be served for their money in the capacity of whites were being served. They would enter such businesses, such as restaurants, when blacks were only allowed to receive their services through an outside window. These students would take up unoccupied stools at the counter of such establishments where they would humbly request to be served, and though their efforts to end segregation in the South in a humble manner only resulted in the students being severely beaten, after which, they would be hauled off to jail for their participation in a nonviolent movement for civil rights.

College students from all around the country began to flood the South as they sympathized with what the college students in the South were enduring, all in the name of justice. The northern, eastern, and western kids, while knowing what they were walking into, with many being white, placed their lives and safety on the line as they courageously adventured the deep South to join these "sit-ins." More than seventy thousand students across the South and the country became involved in the civil rights movement. And though they were beaten repeatedly and, after which, would even be hauled off to jail, they never fought back! It was during the time of these "sit-ins," nevertheless that the students who refused to allow fear or intimidation to stop them later invented the "freedom rides," in which they would board interstate buses and take up the front seats of the buses that were preserved for whites only.

Colored people were to be seated at the back of the buses. And just as with the "sit-ins," the participants of the "freedom rides" all received the same violent and inhumane treatment. From the "freedom rides" was born "Mississippi Summer" by these students. And even though they were constantly being beaten, jailed, and making no progress with the white supremacists of the South, "Mississippi Summer" had been about these students adventuring the Deep South during one summer in their efforts to encourage the fearful southern citizens to go out to the polls and cast their votes. They would even escort the fearful citizens to be registered and then later to the poll where they would attempt to cast their votes because, during these times, there were blacks who had been beaten and killed for even trying to register to vote. During that horrific summer, however, which has gone down in history known as "Mississippi summer," three of these courageous students (may their souls rest in peace) were found murdered by the southern whites for their involvement in the voting activities.

The three students that had been killed, two of which were white and the third being black, were all natives of other parts of the country. All three had been traveling in a vehicle in an excluded area of the state (Mississippi) when they were pursued by their killers, who at some point managed to stop their vehicle from overpowering these students. After that, they had been reported missing, and an extreme search went underway; their bodies were eventually discovered inside their vehicle, which had been pulled from the bottom of a river. The two white students that were involved, however, had been discovered to have sustained a single gunshot wound each, executional-style to their heads. But the black student had been beaten beyond recognition, tortured, and shot several times in the head and through the heart. Just to name a few of the brutal realities that African-Americans faced during those awful times of racial segregation, the injustice and brutality did not stop here, with so many black men, women, and children being killed and beaten beyond recognition by the Southern whites in unbelievable numbers.

On the other hand, the authorities did not only participate in the "unlawful" killings and beatings of blacks, but they also stood by and literally watched while, in most cases, never making an arrest or a conviction. This was because the courts were plainly emphasizing that it was justice rather than a crime when white Americans murdered a black man in cold blood. Dr. King, on December 10, 1964, became the youngest person ever to receive the Nobel Peace Prize. And in his acceptance speech, which he gave in Oslo, Norway, he stated that he was receiving the award as "a trustee for the twenty-two million Negroes in the United States of America who are engaged in a created battle to end the night of racial injustice." The Supreme Court ruling in 1946 that made segregation on interstate buses illegal (a federal law) also entered a ruling that made segregation in public businesses illegal as well. It was because of these laws that Southern blacks were given the right to vote, to be seated in the front section of interstate buses, and to be served in the same capacity in public businesses as Southern whites. It was because these laws were passed that inspired and compelled college students of all races from around the country to take a courageous stand against the injustice of the South. A stand that many brave men, women, and children had been willing to die for, and unfortunately, many of them did!

They laid down their lives so that you and I can walk in the many opportunities today, which, through the stand they took, have been made possible! Ordinary people who have conquered the extraordinary, and for this, I am forever grateful, which is why I have dedicated a portion of this book to the true icons, legends, and patrons for the sacrifices that they have made and for the legacy they have left behind! Due to the enthusiasm of the white segregationists in maintaining segregation throughout the South, I'm convinced that if it had not been for the courageous stand taken by these heroes, segregation would still exist in the South today. And as such, I will always be indebted to them! Because if it had not been for the path laid before us by them, we would not be where we are today! So, in honor of them all, let us never forget the many grueling battles and atrocities that they endured for our freedom and equality!

The difficulties and struggles of today are but the price we must pay for the accomplishments and victories of tomorrow. (Williams J. H. Boetcker)

We must learn to live together as brothers or die together as fools. (Dr. Martin Luther King Jr.)

Now, speaking of the day that has gone down in history known as "Mississippi summer," I just happen to be a native Mississippian, which, during those times, is said to have been the worst in the

South where racial segregation had been at its hardest! But I am proud to note that although racism is still alive in America today, things in Mississippi are no longer that way. And truth be told, in most places today, you will find that whites will sometimes treat you with more dignity than the members of your own race. However, it was around the age of eight that I can vividly remember hearing grownups speaking of a horrific occurrence that transpired right in my very own hometown. The incident surrounded an African-American female who, during the time, could have been considered an alcoholic. And it may have been the result of her having consumed too much alcohol that dared her to adventure into a white establishment (bar).

Now, I do not know exactly what age she was at the time, but I do know that she was in her twenties. However, when her father (may his soul rest in peace) learned of her whereabouts through someone who had witnessed her enter the bar, out of fear for her safety, he disregarded his own when he entered the all-white establishment to bring his daughter out from among a bunch of drunken racist white men. He bravely entered the establishment as he searched for his daughter, and when he located her, he attempted to escort her away when his effort to do so was hindered by some of the white men in the bar. He was ordered to leave the bar without his daughter, and after refusing to abandon her, he was then overpowered by several of the white men inside the bar, where they violently dealt with him. When his remains were eventually found, he had been badly lynched. His private part had been amputated and stuffed inside his mouth, whereas the remainder of his body had been cut into little pieces and placed inside a sackcloth, which had been thrown into a nearby creek. I had heard this described by adults many times while growing up around 1976. During this time, being only eight years old, I was smart enough to fully grasp the horror of it all, while on the other hand, my young, undeveloped mind wasn't nearly mature enough to even begin to comprehend the racial aspect of what had occurred.

It was also around this age that I can vividly remember hearing the grownups speaking of the many boycotts that took place in communities during these times. It was said that the blacks in our town were forbidding other blacks from entering any business that didn't seem to treat blacks with the same respect and dignity that were given to the white race. And if any blacks attempted to enter such business that was being "boycotted," then they would either be beaten even before having a chance to enter the establishment or upon exiting it and have their bags full of groceries ripped from their hands and scattered all along the street by the "black boycotters."

It was because of the segregation of the South that many blacks migrated to other parts of the country, such as Chicago, New York, Detroit, etc., just to escape the oppression of the South and where they would have had a greater opportunity for employment and success. Think of what it would be like if you were white all your life in America during these times, and suddenly, one day, you were black. You had always known there was racism out there, but you never knew how awful it was until you were black. I mean, it is horrifying to truly grasp what it was really like to be black in America just sixty years ago. But it is fascinating to look back on the struggle of blacks in the South, both for the picture, it paints of what we endured and for the light it throws on so much that we have since accomplished.

And although it is necessary that we look toward the future, it is also critical that our young people be aware of and understand the past. One thing that we should never forget about, never eradicate from our memories, is what they have suffered because of the opportunities that exist today!

As African Americans, we have a historical obligation and duty to carry on the legacy and struggle of our ancestors. And my sincerest gratitude goes out to each of the brave men, women, and children who, with all their hearts, soul, and courage, put their lives on the line not only for the cause of racial and human justice but for a better America. And however harsh this account of the civil rights movement may appear, it still doesn't come close to what the American slaves endured in this country.

I don't want to forget about them and what they went through, which account of such can be seen clearly in the Narrative of Frederick Douglass, an autobiography of his early life as an American slave, which he wrote shortly after his escape, published in 1845. You will be taken aback by this dramatic account of slavery that was written 175 years ago today, and within only seven years of his escape, him being unable to read, write, or spell at the time of his escape with such knowledge being forbidden to slaves who were not even permitted by slave matters to read the Holy Bible! But this goes on to say that not all white people are alike in their thinking. In fact, there were many throughout the country, including the South, who supported the cause of civil rights and couldn't be held accountable for what their people did during those times, and neither can anyone be today!

In fact, there are some decent-hearted whites in the world today, just as there are some evil-hearted blacks in the world today! But the reality of it is that although things have changed in America, racism is not gone. The violence between blacks and whites is not gone. But what we can say as a nation is that today's situation isn't anything like it was just fifty or sixty years ago.

Getting back to the young prisoner I was sharing this knowledge with in the beginning. I informed him after sharing it with him that being his age, there is no reason why he shouldn't have known of this significant but tragic part of history. And that being a black man, it was a shame that he didn't, and sadly, there are many who are so often ignorant of their own heritage. I tried to encourage him, nevertheless, to stop filling his head with a bunch of negative ideals and to seek to learn of such things instead because knowledge is power, and you must know where you come from in order to know where you are going. Because in today's world, it is all too common to see freedom lost through ignorance.

Many civil rights legends have died so that we can live freely and have a say in how our government works. And the cruel and inhumane murders that were perpetrated only represent what they died fighting against. Although they're gone, the great pioneers' legacy lives on! We must never lose focus; it is through our children that we keep the dream alive, even though it may appear that without these icons, the struggle to overcome has ceased among us. It is through our children that we will push on, we will persevere, and we will overcome!

I remember staring out of my cell window one day in amazement at two small birds that had built their nest on top of a pole, which at the top of it was mounted a surveillance camera that had a little tin roof to protect the camera from the weather. I watched as one of the birds would fly off, only to return after a period of about twenty minutes carrying some type of food in its beak as it would land under the little tin roof of the camera, which was where their nest had been built. And no sooner did it land in the nest than the other bird immediately flew away in the same direction that the arriving bird had gone and returned from.

Captivated by it, I watched them continue this sequence for hours, taking turns hunting for food while safeguarding their young in the nest from predators. And sure enough, as I continued to watch, a huge black crow appeared out of nowhere and landed on top of the tin roof that covered the bird's nest. It stood about two feet away from the nest, with the nest being hidden beneath the structure out of plain sight. It was as if the crow had sensed its presence with the little baby birds or eggs in it. Now, it was clear to me from the beginning that the mother or father bird that was in the nest, guarding it from predators, was aware of the crow's intrusion. But it wasn't until the crow had made its attempt to invade the nest that the little bird swiftly exited it and attacked its intruder, even though it was eight times its size! And at first, the crow endured the attack and made no attempts to decline its desire to invade the nest. But with the much smaller bird's "life or death" aggression, it had no choice but to surrender and fly away!

The moral of the story is, if these little creatures were protective enough of their young to have taken turns safeguarding them in the nest, as fathers, should we be any less protective of our children? We shouldn't want our children to supplicate, to be raised by the streets, or to grow old in prison! It is trust that there are certain things in life that should always remain one's prerogative, but the choice of whether to be a parent to our children, however, should never become a decision with today's youth's needing someone to look up to, someone to imitate. June 15 is a special day that honors men. But to be real men, we must first accept our responsibilities as fathers. So, as men, we must father our children in this time of crisis and not let them continue to fall by the wayside!

# PART 5

## Awesome Savior

We're living in a dark age where hatred, evil, jealousy, and a disregard for human life are on a rampage! Now more than ever, we need God in our lives. Jesus, which means "The Lord saves," Immanuel, "God with us," and Messiah, "Savior," all point to him as the "Sacrificial Lamb" of God. "For no one can lay a foundation other than that which is laid, which is Jesus Christ" (1 Cor. 3:11). In this part of the book, I would like to share with you my vision of such matters that has been prophesied to take place in the book of Revelation, which has left me with the assurance of two most certain facts: "God is most definitely real, as the Scriptures has proclaimed him to be. In fact, the complexity in the design of living things alone provides inexplicable evidence for a creator" (Heb. 3:12). This warns us to "take heed, brethren, lest there be in any of you an evil heart of unbelief, in departing from the living God. And secondly, God has a calling on my life in aiding the gospel of Christ."

You see, God will sometimes use many different methods to attract our undivided attention whether it's through people, places, things, events, or even, sometimes, dreams! Part 5 of this book has been inspired by several dreams I had. But let's not forget that God works in mysterious ways that cannot be known by the wicked because they are spiritually discerned. Nevertheless, I don't usually remember my dreams, but I would wake up with these particularly vivid in mind. I am positive that many of us have seen a portrait of the crucifixion of Christ at one time or another.

Well, this fixed image of the Lord came to me in a dream around the year 1992; however, I know that there are some people who do not accept the image given in the crucifixion portrait of Christ as being Christ, and my aim is not to debate such notions, for I do not worship my Lord in the flesh but in the spirit. I truly believe the reason why God revealed his Son to me in the exact image given in the crucifixion portrait is perhaps due to my upbringing as a young Baptist who recognized the image of Christ as being the Son of God. In order to see someone and recognize them for who they are, you would at least first have to have a prevision of that person. In this dream, I was accompanied by another as we journeyed across the type of foundation that would be best described by comparing it to an enormous ranch.

There were weeds and grass of various types as far as your eyes could see, and this is to exclude sidewalks, paved streets, or any kind of buildings or facilities. And as the two of us adventured along while engaging in conversations, I was soon distracted by what appeared to be some sort of descending object. Captivated by the sight of what I was seeing, I pointed it out to my companion as we both stood observing this descending object as it drew closer to land. And as it came into view, the first detail I noticed was the figure of a human being, but still so far away that the distinctive features of the individual could not be identified by the naked eye. But as it continued to descend, we were soon able to identify this individual as our Lord and Savior, Jesus Christ!

Having the exact characteristics of the image of Christ given in the crucifixion portrait and having descended approximately ten feet in between himself and us, Jesus held up one finger as he gestured for us to approach him. As we neared him, the very first words he spoke were, "Mark this spot." Immediately, we fell to our knees with a mind of marking the space in between Jesus's feet, wondering how a writing marker supernaturally appeared within our hands as we went down, and it's no coincidence that of all things, a "cross" came to mind in being used as the symbol to mark the spot with. Having marked the straight line of the cross, we were about to mark the "cross" line to complete it when Jesus stated, "Keep it clean." I did not fully understand the significance of being asked to keep such a small area clean when, as far as the eyes could see in either direction, there were grass and weeds of all sorts. Since the Lord knows our every thought even before the heart could conceive them, he knew that this mystery had us puzzled. And as we stared at each other in a state of confusion, the Lord then stated, "For where I stand is Holy ground." And there could not have been given a more significant reason for keeping that little spot "clean" than what the Lord had given!

When I awakened the next morning, my spirit was deeply troubled as to why I had dreamed such a dream and how it was meant to comply with my life. Immediately, I arose from the bed to obtain my Bible. I then began to listen to the inner spirit as it instructed me in interpreting the dream. Revelation 2:17 says, "He that has an ear, let him hear what the Spirit saith unto the churches." I could literally hear the Spirit speaking to me as it instructed me to "place your fingers into the outer pages of the Bible and open it, and whatever page, chapter, or verse that catches your immediate slight, there, begin to read." As I followed the instructions given by the Holy Spirit, I came across the Scripture that reads, "Know ye not that ye are the temple of God, and that the Spirit of God dwelleth in you? If any man defile the temple of God, him shall God destroy; for the temple of God is holy, which temple ye are" (1 Cor. 3:16–17).

It's obvious that this Scripture does, in fact, correspond with the dream. This Scripture being interpreted is saying that "God has desired my body to become the temple of the Holy Spirit, as it warns of the importance of keeping it clean. Because sin cannot dwell in God's presence, nor can God dwell in the presence of sin!" Having read this Scripture, it was obvious that God was dealing with me. Enthusiastically, I longed for further insight. Since I was incarcerated at the time of dreaming this dream, I frequently attended church sermons during the week. It was there that I felt compelled to seek further interpretation of my dream through the many different ministers who would take turns in their coming to share God's Word.

After sharing my dream with several of the pastors who came over the course of time, I found one communion that stands out the most among the interpretations that were given by these pastors. The pastor said to me, "Young man, God has a calling on your life in aiding the gospel of Christ. The Bible says, 'At the name of Jesus every knee shall bow, of things in heaven, and things in earth, and things under the earth' (Phil. 2:10–11). Young man, you have already bowed at the feet of Jesus, and my encouragement to you is to keep yourself there." God's agenda is to bring all things together in Christ until every knee bows before him.

There was another dream in 1992, and in this dream, I was accompanied by three others as we sat conversing, surrounding a table in the front room of a house, when suddenly, from the outside came the rushing sound of a trumpet that could be heard throughout the inside of the entire house. Curious as to who may have been blowing the trumpet, in haste, the four of us exited the house and were now standing on the front porch, but to our amazement, there was no one there. Leaping from the porch, while assuming that there must have been someone around the side of the house, having heard the trumpet being blown, to our astonishment, there was no one there as well. It was then that we realized the trumpet was in fact being blown from the heavens above. This means that the entire sky was completely sounding off when the trumpet was blowing (Rev. 8:1–6).

Having witnessed this phenomenon, the four of us reentered the house, and as the last man to enter pulled the door shut behind him, immediately, midday turned into black darkness, followed by heavy rain, lightning, and thundering (Rev. 16:10). The lightning was so intense that we all fell to our knees, engrossed by the fear of what was happening. There was occasional lightning with such ferociousness that it caused the entire house to brighten as if it had still been a day on the outside that lasted for only seconds consecutively but seemed like hours. It was as though the lightning just hung across the sky, and the sound of the trumpet continued to blow. I tried to escape the reality of the dream by crawling into an area of the house where there may have been fewer windows, but only to realize just how impossible it will be to escape the wrath of God on the day of judgment because, in this room, there were fewer windows, true enough, but the intensity of the lightning was still the same.

Revelation 6:15–17 speaks, "The day of judgment approaches, men will try to seek out ways to avoid God's wrath, even unto death." Having acknowledged this fact, it was then that the rain, lightning, and thunder ceased, and the brightness of the day simultaneously reappeared (but the sound of the trumpet continued to blow). For the second time, the four of us exited the house as we stood on the ground gazing into the clouds in astonishing amazement at the trumpet being blown. Suddenly, in the center of the sky, the clouds began to depart in a rolling motion in all four directions (Rev. 6:14). The results were that a door had been opened in heaven, by which four angels appeared out of. See the account given by John in Revelation 4:1, which says, "After this, I looked, and, behold, a door was opened in heaven: and the first voice which I heard was as if it were of a trumpet talking with me, which said, 'Come up hither, and I will shew thee things which must be hereafter.'" Revelation 7:1 also says, "And after these things I saw four angels standing on the four corners of the Earth, holding the four winds of the earth, that the wind should not blow on the earth, nor on the sea, nor on any tree."

The angels begin to descend and ascend continually, and each time they ascend, they would descend lower than the previous time before. The angels kept repeating this cycle until they had become low enough that their appearances could easily be recognized. Their appearances were as if they were bright clouds with a darker shade about their edge that gave the angels the image of a human being but with wings. Having witnessed the sight of the angels, the four of us reentered the house, and as in the first instance, after the last man that entered pulled the door shut behind him, immediately the daylight turned into black darkness, followed by heavy rain, lightning, and thundering, and the sound of the trumpet continued to blow.

Likewise, we fell into a prostrate position consumed by fear. Being on my knees, I began to pray, "Dear Lord, I am a sinner. Please forgive me of my sins and save me." And after praying this prayer and realizing that the reality of the dream still remained, I simply repeated it for the second time, "Dear Lord, I am a sinner. Please forgive me of my sins and save me." Instantaneously, after repeating the payer for the second time, it was then as if something had awakened me out of the dream. Romans 10:13 says, "For whosoever shall call upon the name of the Lord shall be saved."

There was another dream in 1992 as well, and in this dream, I could see that there was a white Bible with the words "Holy Bible" written on it in bold red letters, which lingered at a distance of a foot away from my face as I slept. The characteristics of the Bible were so intense that I could have compared them to a needle being constantly poked into my flesh as if to demand my attention. The brightness of the Bible was as if the sun shined in its strength, and the whiteness of its color was as white as snow.

After I had awakened from this dream, the very first thing I did was to retrieve my Bible, and being led by the spirit, I came across the Scripture that read, "And one of the elders answered, saying unto me, What are these which are arrayed in white robes? And whence came they? And I said unto him, Sir, thou knowest. And he said to me, These are they which came out of great tribulation, and have washed their robes, and made them white in the blood of the Lamb" (Rev. 7:13–14).

The bold red letters in the dream represented the Blood of the Lamb in the Scripture. The whiteness of the Bible's color in the dream represented the "white robes" that were given to the saints in the scripture. And the extremely "bright glow" of the Bible represents the countenance of Jesus's face in Revelation 1:16, which says, "And he had in his right hand seven stars: and out of his mouth went a sharp two-edged sword: and his countenance was as the sun shineth in his strength." My interpretation of this dream is that I've been ordained to aid the gospel of Christ through God's Word, the Holy Bible.

There was another dream somewhere around the nineties as well, and in this dream, there was me and two others as the three of us were all indulging in a game of cards, when suddenly, a stranger approached the table and stated, "While y'all are sitting here playing cards, you need to be getting your houses in order," the stranger warned.

But in spite of his warnings, he was asked, "Who are you to tell us that we need to be getting our houses in order when you are just a common man as we are?"

We were overwhelmed by laughter when the stranger replied, "I am an angel," and as we continued ridiculing the stranger, he then stated, "I haven't come to force you into believing that I am an angel. But I have come only to deliver the message." With the facility walls being constructed out of cinder blocks that are made from cement and coal cinders, the stranger began to ascend in midair until he reached the ceiling, where he then began to remove cinder blocks from the top portion of the wall by simply reaching out and taking them into his arms, one after another until he had taken three of them despite the fact that they had all been carefully cemented in place!

And it soon became obvious that this stranger wasn't just an ordinary man as we had assumed, as the mockery came to a cease and the curiosity sat in. Having descended back down to the floor, as well as having gained everyone's attention, the stranger began to place one cinder block directly in front of each of us as he demanded that we should not touch them until he had been given the order to do so. And as he would set each cinder block onto the table, it would immediately be transformed in to a tablet of stone. The stranger then pointed toward the first of us as he commanded us to "Flip over your stone and read the writing thereof." As the first of us, as instructed by the stranger, frantically turned over his stone, his writing in it read, "Hell will be your home!" Then, straightforwardly, the stranger pointed toward the second man, indicating that it was now his turn to flip over his stone.

He hesitated to do so after witnessing the results of the first man's stone, but as if by some force that left him no choice, he nervously flipped over his stone. When he did, the writing in it revealed that

"You have a slight chance of entering God's kingdom."

As I sat discouraged, observing the reading of the two men before me, the stranger then made gestures in my direction, indicating that it was now my turn to flip over the stone. As I reached out in fear of what the writing may have revealed, it was then that instantaneously, as I had taken hold of the stone while in the process of flipping it over, something had awakened me out of the dream. Hebrew 13:2 warns us, "Be not forgetful to entertain stranger: for thereby some have entertained angels unawares."

But my interpretation of this dream is that God's judgment will surely come against the ungodly. Revelation 20:12 says, "And I saw the dead, small and great, stand before God; and the books were opened: and another book was opened, which is the were judged out of those things which were written in the books, according to their works." Today is the day of salvation! Tomorrow just very well may be too late! Hell is full of people who are waiting for a more convenient time!

Why, just last night, I had a dream that was perhaps the shortest of all dreams. And in this dream, I dreamed that I had died, but right at the point of death, I could literally feel and see my soul departing from my flesh with such realism that it jolted me awake! This revelation has assured me that death is not a one-way street; it is simply an expressway to heaven or hell! This is why the apostle Paul stated, "To die is to gain, to a born-again Christian." But also, we find in the account of John in Revelation 20:12 that the dead shall stand before God at judgment. For it is by the unmerited favor of God that we are saved and delivered from judgment and have been made partakers of Christ's salvation, and this salvation is not of yourselves or of your own doing, but it is the gift of God unto all that believe.

The writer of Hebrew 4:3 tells us, "For we who have believed do enter that rest." God sets himself against the proud, the insolent, the overbearing, the disdainful, and the boastful but gives grace to the humble. In this next dream, however, I dreamed that I was at home alone right before deciding to exit the house. But as I approached the front door to open it, much to my surprise, there were approximately eight demons. Some had been sitting on buckets while others had been stretched out all over my front porch, and at the threshold laid the carcass of a dog that had begun to decay, which the demons who had obviously placed there and were all gathered surrounding it.

Since I didn't realize at first that my visitors were, in fact, demons and not humans, I began to question them regarding their presence, and being that they only stared at me as if unable to speak, it was then that I began to examine my encounters closely. Their appearance was as if someone had died and was buried, and right after their body had begun to decay, they were freed from their graves. Having established the true identity and nature of my unwelcomed guests, I decided that I would leave the house without giving it a second thought to return! But demons are persistently aggressive because after clearing the distance of maybe a hundred yards from the house, I noticed that one of the demons had begun to chase me. As soon as it had become within arm's reach of me, I forced it into a headlock as I began to pound it with my fist, and when I thought that it had become weak enough, I pushed it aside and fled. Instantly, its strength revived as it grabbed hold of me, but somehow, I managed to free myself of it and ran. But this persistent demon continued to chase me until I awakened out of the dream.

Ephesians 6:12 warns us, "For we wrestle not against flesh and blood, but against principalities, against powers, against the rulers of the darkness of this world, against spiritual wickedness in high places." Now the Scriptures solemnly warn us, "To take extreme precaution in regarding the fact that our adversary the devil has come down unto us, having great wrath seeking who he may devour" (1 Pet. 5:8), which brings me to my next dream, because in it, God has revealed Satan unto me! However, in this dream, Satan was seen floating across the open sky as he eventually drifted out of sight. Satan's appearance was as if he had been made from what appeared to be pure black smoke, and his dimension was gigantic. The smoke that formed his image had truly been blacker than oil as he floated across mid-sky in this dream. The characteristics of his image were that there was about him, two bull-like horns that protruded from either side of his forehead, two arms, two legs, as well as a tail, and he carried in his hand a three-pointed fork, as I observed him vanish away in the distance.

The Bible tells of a rich man who died and was buried, and on the hill, he lifted up his eyes. Immediately, without warning, without any escape, without any hope, he was in hell. Satan's most powerful deception, perhaps, is to deceive men into thinking that he doesn't exist. Revelation 20:10 says, "And the devil that deceived them was cast into the lake of fire and brimstone, where the beast and the false prophet are, and shall be tormented day and night forever and ever." Why, just last night, I had a dream, and in it, there was me and three others as we gathered together to have lunch when I began to inquire if any of them would have been interested in exchanging a watch for a ring since I didn't have a watch and would have preferred one over the ring.

Unfortunately, there was no one who was interested in making the trade. Now, as we began to have lunch, one of the men tried to convince me that I should seek revenge against someone who he felt may have wronged me. And as he was speaking, that's when I spotted a beautiful watch lying in the nearby grass. Having finished my meal, I casually made my way across the distance to obtain my blessing. It was an elegant gold-plated watch with a leather band and diamonds in it. Taking the watch into my hands, it was then that I began to speak to the men in the dream,

To everything, there is a season and a time for every purpose under the heaven: A time to be born, and a time to die; a time to plant, and a time to pluck up that which is planted; A time to kill, and a time to heal; a time to break down, and a time to build up; a time to weep, and a time to laugh; a time to mourn, and a time to dance; A time to cast away stones, and a time to gather stones together; a time to embrace, and a time to refrain from embracing; A time to get, and a time to lose; a time to keep, and a time to cast away; a time to rend, and a time to sew; a time to keep silence, and a time to speak; A time to love, and a time to hate; a time of war, and a time of peace. (Eccles. 3:1–8)

And it's ironic that as I awakened this morning, the very first thought that entered my mind was, "He's an on-time God! Yes, he is!" The fact that this dream has truly been one of a divine cannot be disputed simply because you see, the watch in the dream does, in fact, correspond with the biological time of nature that the Scripture has proclaimed that "In time all things must take place."

God, in his awesome timing, has revealed yet another revelation to me. In this dream, on what appeared to be an ordinary day, there were people who were engaging in the normal activities of life. Suddenly, out of the clear blue sky, it began to rain! The sky turned darker and darker, and although it had become extremely darkened for that hour of the day, there was yet an odd but brilliant illumination about it. And as such, it enabled me to distinguish "the first sheep!" It was midway in the sky and was fashioned from the clouds as it traveled in a 360-degree circle around the globe! And it was as if I had been watching it from a giant projector screen. This huge sheep, which suddenly appeared out of nowhere, had just as suddenly disappeared. And it is difficult to describe the "realism" of my first brief sight of it! I stood there, not knowing what to expect next or if I had others seen it as well. One huge sheep after another began to appear as they walked in a 360-degree circle around the globe! One after the other!

Now, it became obvious that everyone was aware of the sheep, and as soon as they saw them, they were astounded. As many who had been in fear began to panic, there were people who had begun to scream, cry, and run in every direction! But as I stood there, both captivated and frightened, I expected to see Jesus appear at any second! And it was during this highly anticipated moment that I was awakened out of the dream! After I had awakened from the dream, however, and sought insight from God and his guidance, there is no doubt that our gracious Father has shared with me yet another phenomenal and miraculous vision that surrounds the fact that Jesus Christ is the "humble Lamb" of God (John 1:29), who is also the "Good Shepherd" (john 10:11), which is soon to return to gather his flock!"

And in an increasingly chaotic world, what a hopeful thought that Jesus could return at any moment. More comforting still is the anticipation that all who trust him for salvation will be raptured, as members of the church, to live with the Lord forever! (Heb. 9:28; Titus 2:13–14). When you think about it, the two most important events that will ever occur in this world are the first being Jesus Christ being born into this world to save sinners and the second the return of Jesus to rapture the church! Hallelujah!

The soul without Christ is in great danger! Friend, if you are still an unbelieving sinner, you are in a terrible state and on your way to terrible doom! "He that believes on the Son hath everlasting life: and he that believed not the Son shall not see life, but the wrath of God abideth on him" (John 3:36). Escape to Christ, trust in him, and then you will not perish while the breath of God remains in you. Having witnessed such insights of God's revelation, it's no wonder that this book was predestined to be written, having been ordained by God from the beginning of creation; it's no coincidence that I have dreamed these dreams.

Acts 2:17–18 says, "And it shall come to pass in the last days, said God, I will pour out of my Spirit upon all flesh: and your sons and your daughters shall prophesy, and your young men shall see vision, and your old men shall dream dreams: And on my servants and on my handmaidens I will pour out in those days of my Spirit; and they shall prophesy." Neither are there any doubts in my faith pertaining to the significance thereof: "For God speaketh once, yea twice, yet man perceiveth it not. In a dream, in a vision of the night, when deep sleep falleth upon men, in slumberings upon the bed; then he opens the ears of men, and sealeth their instruction" (Job 33:14–16).

This evidence in support of the things that have been prophesied to take place in the book of Revelation is clear. I'm not a dreamer of prophetic dreams, and have God not given the prophetic revelations which I have shared? If you have a dream, stand by it. Never give anyone the power to take away your dream! My dream has been to share these visions with as many as God wills, and for this, I am eternally grateful! Proverbs 29:18 says, "Where there is no vision, the people perish."

God's messengers warned the people to repent during the days of Lot and Noah. Likewise, I am warning the readers that we are living in the last days before Christ's return, and I'm ever conscious of what the Lord has called me to do. When God's call did come, I responded not only with the messages that God gave me to proclaim but with testimonies of my own to share. In my next dream, which God revealed to me following this one, there were a number of others, and I gathered about what also appeared to be a beautiful and normal day. Now, I didn't recognize these people in the dream, as was the case of all of the dreams, for some reason. However, the people and I were gathered about, each minding his/her own business, when suddenly, the fire began to zoom from the sky! And though everyone acknowledged the fire falling down from heaven as it landed only in the streets with great force and speed! Yet they appeared oblivious to this fact, as the asphalt was instantly ignited in huge huffs of fire. And even I was dumbfounded by the fire until the second instance of fire that had fallen, which caused the full reality of it all to sit in. And being able to discern that everyone else was still not certain of this reality, it was then that I began to testify to the destruction of Sodom and Gomorrah. Genesis 19:23–24 reads, "The sun was risen upon the earth when Lot entered into Zo'ar. Then the Lord rained upon Sodom and upon Gomorrah brimstone and fire from the Lord out of heaven."

I begin to testify in the dream that "the end of time" is near anytime that God has allowed fire to fall from heaven upon the Earth… as were in the days of Sodom and Gomorrah! And it has been a privilege and an honor to be used by God in sharing these revelations that he has revealed to me! You see, God is not only willing to use the foolish things of the world to confound the wise. He is a God who is also able to turn our adversities into opportunities and to create a 360-degree turnaround of our lives and image! "And that, knowing the time, that now it is high time to awake out of sleep: for now is our salvation nearer than when we believed" (Rom. 13:11). And "Today, if you hear his voice, do not harden your hearts" (Heb. 4:7). It is from the ground that our

Creator and provider have caused food to grow on trees. It is from the ground that our Creator has caused food to grow on vines. It is from the ground, then, that we are nurtured. And it is from the ground that we were created, and that is where we shall all someday return! Will you be ready?

# ABOUT THE AUTHOR

Adrian Maurice Jenkins is a humble and God-fearing man. He knows that man is not a perfect being, but he strives for the best in everything he does and believes in. He wholeheartedly puts his trust in the Almighty God.

The author has been released from prison since August 2020. He currently resides in his hometown of Louise, Mississippi, and has now purchased his own home and continues his writing endeavors.

Made in the USA
Monee, IL
04 November 2026

67382304R00066